Collins *practical g*

BULBS

Collins *practical gardener*

BULBS

GEOFF HODGE

First published in 2005 by HarperCollins*Publishers*

77–85 Fulham Palace Road, London, W6 8JB

The Collins website address is:

www.collins.co.uk

Text by Geoff Hodge; copyright © HarperCollins*Publishers*

Artworks and design © HarperCollins*Publishers*

The majority of photographs in this book were taken by
Tim Sandall. A number of other images were supplied
by David Sarton.

Cover photography by Tim Sandall

Photographic props: Coolings Nurseries, Rushmore Hill,
Knockholt, Kent, TN14 7NN, www.coolings.co.uk

Design and editorial: Focus Publishing, Sevenoaks, Kent

Project editor: Guy Croton

Editor: Vanessa Townsend

Project co-ordinator: Caroline Watson

Design & illustration: David Etherington

Editorial assistant: George Croton

For HarperCollins

Senior managing editor: Angela Newton

Design manager: Luke Griffin

Editor: Alastair Laing

Assistant editor: Lisa John

Production: Chris Gurney

A CIP catalogue record for this book is available from the
British Library

ISBN 0-00-719281-9

Colour reproduction by Colourscan

Printed and bound in Italy by L.E.G.O.

Contents

Introduction

One of the secrets of becoming a good gardener is thinking ahead – planning for the seasons and years to come. And nowhere is this more true than in the world of bulbs. Planting bulbs in autumn for flowers in winter and spring, and in spring for summer and autumn colour is one of the joys of gardening.

Yes, you can buy potted bulbs in leaf, in bud or in flower, but the true experience of bulb growing is buying and planting the dormant bulbs knowing that in a few weeks' or months' time they will burst into growth and produce a display that will bring cheer to the soul and colour to the home or garden.

The excitement of waiting for bulbs to poke through the soil is only matched by that of seeing seeds germinate. And yet bulb growing is so much easier and often more rewarding. Bulbs are the perennial equivalent of the annual bedding plants but, unlike these plants that have to be sown afresh every year, most bulbs can remain in the soil for many years, sitting dormant until it's time to burst into growth and adorn the garden again.

Gardeners sometimes struggle to find plants that are suitable for growing in 'difficult' garden situations, but often the answer lies in the world of bulbs. Planting under trees and in front of conifers is often seen to be tricky because the tree's canopy reduces light levels

Tubers, bulbs, corms and rhizomes

and the roots remove much of the available moisture and nutrients. The answer – spring-flowering bulbs which will often have grown, flowered and died back again before the tree comes into leaf and its roots become active. Many drought-loving bulbs will even thrive in front of conifers; for instance, I've seen a fantastic display of nerines growing at the base of a leylandii hedge (X *Cupressocyparis leylandii*).

Although bulbs are often an obvious choice for planting in beds, borders and containers, they can be used in situations where other plants would not be able to cope. Planted in rough grass or in the lawn, they can bring much welcome colour to an area that would otherwise be seen as rather dull. Both rock gardens and even the edges of ponds benefit from generous bulb planting to provide extra flower power. And when the bulb craze gets you firmly in its grip you can use bulbs to bring colour to the house, conservatory and greenhouse, too.

So all you need is a little forward planning, a hint of imagination and a copy of this book to turn your garden or even paved area into a colourful, exciting and enjoyable place all year round.

Colour combinations can be impressive, such as this mix of tulips and hyacinths

How to Use This Book

This book is divided into three parts. The opening chapter introduces you to the types of 'bulbs' available, where to buy them from and what to look out for, how and where to plant them, ways for you to maintain them as they grow into plants, ideas on colour scheme planting, as well as container planting, and general care and attention. A comprehensive plant directory follows, with individual entries on around 100 of the most commonly available bulbs. These are listed in alphabetical order, with an entry showing which 'bulb' type the plant is. The final section of the book covers particular plant problems. Troubleshooting pages allow you to diagnose the likely cause of any problems, and a directory of pests and diseases offers advice on how to solve them.

latin name of the plant genus, followed by its **common name** and what **type** it is

detailed descriptions outline the particular qualities of each plant and give specific care advice

alphabetical tabs on the side of the page, colour-coded to help you quickly find the plant you want

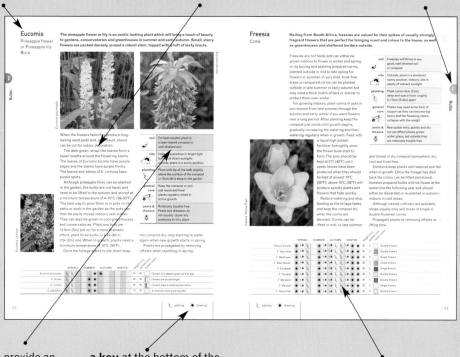

care charts provide an at-a-glance summary of the plant's specific needs

a key at the bottom of the page explains what each symbol means

variety charts list recommended varieties for genera of bulbs that feature more than one variety. These display key information to help you choose your ideal plant, showing:

• when the plant is in flower during the year
• when (or if) the plant needs to be potted up before planting outside
• the height and spread after optimum growth
• the principal colour of the flowers (or foliage)
• additional comments from the author

Bulb Types

Although all the plants in this book are loosely referred to as 'bulbs', not all of them are true bulbs; they may be corms, tubers, rhizomes or tuberous roots. All are underground food storage organs of the plant in question. So what is the difference between them?

Bulb

If you cut through a bulb from top to bottom you will see its structure. The centre of a mature, well-formed true bulb contains an embryonic flower bud, which means it is almost guaranteed to flower in its first year (small and immature bulbs may not be large enough to contain an embryonic flower). Surrounding the embryonic bud is the undeveloped shoot.

The body of the bulb is composed of a number of fleshy scales. These are modified leaves that store the food needed to sustain the plant during its dormant period and early stages of growth, until the true leaves are produced. The scales are attached to a basal plate at the bottom end that holds them in place and from which the roots are produced. In most bulbs the scales are thin and closely packed together, but in others, such as lilies, they are loose and swollen.

Bulbs are propagated by carefully removing the offsets – or bulblets – that are produced around the basal plate.

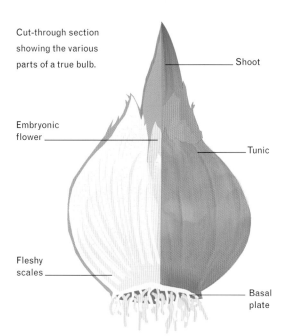

Cut-through section showing the various parts of a true bulb.

- Shoot
- Tunic
- Basal plate
- Fleshy scales
- Embryonic flower

Crocuses emerge from corms

Corm

Many corms look like true bulbs, whereas others are flatter in appearance and do not have a protective tunic. Corms are solid and not composed of fleshy scales, the food storage organ being a swollen stem base. Corms contain one or more central growing points at the top and a basal plate at the bottom from where the roots grow out.

Many corms are covered in a protective tunic that may be smooth or fibrous. This is made up from the dry leaf bases from the previous year.

One of the major differences between bulbs and corms is that corms last just one year, whereas nearly all bulbs last for several years. When the plant starts to grow the food reserves are used up and the corm starts to shrivel and die. At the same time a new corm forms at the top of the old corm, together with a number of smaller corms called cormlets. So although the original corm you planted usually dies, its replacement by new cormlets means there will be more plants the following year.

Tuber

A tuber is an underground swollen stem that stores the plant's food. It has neither a basal plate nor a protective tunic, and the buds or eyes are not neatly arranged in one place but can arise anywhere on the tuber's surface. This means stems can appear from the sides as well as the top, and tubers can produce several stems at once. Roots can appear anywhere along its surface.

Some tubers get larger as the plant develops and grows, whereas others may use up their stored food reserves and start to shrink. With the 'shrinkers' new tubers develop throughout the growing season, which will produce the new plant the following year.

Propagation is usually through dividing the tuber ensuring each piece contains at least one eye or bud.

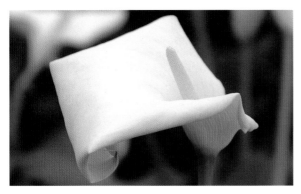

Eranthis hyemalis (winter aconite) grows from a tuber

Zantedeschia aethiopica comes from a rhizome

Rhizome

Like corms and tubers, rhizomes are also swollen underground stems that store food to feed the developing plant, the difference being that rhizomes grow horizontally either partially or completely below ground level.

EXAMPLES OF 'BULB' TYPES
Bulbs Examples include Allium, Fritillaria, Hippeastrum, Hyacinthus, Lilium, Muscari, Narcissus, Tulipa
Corms Examples include Colchicum, Crocosmia, Crocus, Freesia, Ixia, Gladiolus
Tubers Examples include Anemone, Begonia, Cyclamen, Eranthis
Rhizomatous Examples include Achimenes, Agapanthus, Canna, Schizostylis, Zantedeschia
Tuberous root Examples include Alstroemeria, Dahlia, Eremurus, Ranunculus

The main growing point is at the tip of the rhizome but others appear along its length so, like a tuber, several shoots can appear at once. The roots appear from the underside of the rhizome.

Rhizomes are propagated by cutting them into lengths, ensuring each length has at least one bud.

Tuberous root

These structures are large, swollen roots – as opposed to stems or fleshy scales – that the plant uses to store its food reserves. They are produced as a cluster at the base of the stems.

When the plant starts into growth fibrous roots are produced on the swollen roots and it is these that absorb water and nutrients from the soil and store it in the tuberous roots. Over time the roots increase in size or number.

These plants are propagated by carefully cutting off individual roots, at the same time ensuring each has a growing point at the top.

Alstroemeria starts life as a tuberous root

Buying Bulbs

Many bulb species come with the full potential to flower – they should have the flower buds already within them, so first-year flowering should always be a certainty.

Some of the plants in this book are also available as potted plants already in growth. Some, such as Cyclamen, Eranthis and Galanthus, do not always grow successfully from dried bulbs, so it is far better to buy plants in growth. When buying these, always check the plants are looking strong and healthy – the parts above ground, as well as the root system.

Where to buy

The advantage of buying loose bulbs is that you can choose the bulbs you want; always try and pick the biggest and best quality. You may have to take pot luck and hope for the best with those that are packed unless you can check over the individual bulbs in the pack.

Mail order Although most mail order suppliers are reputable, you have to trust they are providing you with the biggest and best they have.

A good way to select bulbs is individually

BUYING TIPS

- Always buy the biggest and best bulbs you can afford.
- Buying large bargain packs of small bulbs may seem a good idea at the time, until they fail to flower!
- Buy your bulbs early in the season, even if you are not ready to plant them. This way you will get the best selection and the bulbs won't have been handled too many times.
- Late season bargain bulbs should be planted immediately. They are likely to have started into growth and although this isn't necessarily a disaster, you should expect some failures.
- Always look for 'Grown from cultivated stocks' on the label. Some bulb species – Cyclamen is a prime example – have been so extensively gathered from the wild that the stocks are exhausted and, as a result, have become almost extinct.

Garden centres Buying bulbs from a garden centre allows you to pick the bulbs and check them over, so you can see whether they have been properly stored.

Supermarkets Always buy early in the season; being warmer than most garden centres, there is the chance that the bulbs will have deteriorated if you buy them late.

What to look for

Wherever possible give the bulbs a thorough inspection before buying to ensure they look strong and healthy – not always easy if you are buying packaged bulbs. Check the planting material is firm to the touch – giving them a gentle squeeze is permissible but do not squash them!

Look out for any signs of pests, disease and rot – a strong musty smell is a sure sign of disease. Bulbs that are shrivelled, misshapen or otherwise look deformed should be avoided as they are more than likely affected.

Always try to buy bulbs that are dormant; if there are signs of leaf or root growth you may have a bulb that has been kept in warm or even hot conditions, which will certainly affect its subsequent growth.

Handling

Never be rough when handling your bulbs; any damage may lead to rotting or impaired performance. Imagine you are buying fruit and handle with the same care.

Certain bulb species can induce an irritant reaction in some people, especially those who commonly experience allergic reactions, and these are best handled with gloves. Common examples include Arum, Hyacinthus, Iris, Narcissus, Scilla and Tulipa. And some bulb species are toxic, so never put them in your mouth and always wash your hands after handling them. Examples include Arisaema, Arum, Colchicum, Ornithogalum, Scilla and Narcissus. Cases of blood poisoning have also been recorded when people with skin cuts have handled the foliage of daffodils.

Garden centres often have a wide range

Planting

Bulbs that will remain in the ground to flower for many years deserve careful planting, as it is difficult to rectify mistakes afterwards.

Always start by ensuring the bulbs are suitable for where you intend to plant them. You will need to assess whether the site and soil type allows for the correct amount of sun, protection from wind, moisture, drainage and nutrients for optimum growth. Most bulbs are fairly adaptable, but any details of specific conditions are given in the plant directory.

For best results always try and plant your bulbs as soon as possible after purchasing. Planting can be delayed – a good idea if the soil is too dry, too wet or frozen – but ensure the bulbs are kept in a cool yet frost-free, dark, dry place. Those species that produce tubers or fleshy roots should be covered with just-moist compost. But always make sure you plant before they start to shoot or go soft.

For the most dramatic displays it pays to plant large groups of the same species and cultivar; dotting one or two here and there often results in disappointment.

Add fertilizer both at planting and during growth

Soil improvement

Before planting it is important to assess the quality of the soil and, where necessary, improve its structure and nutritional content. Start by digging over the area to be planted and adding compost, composted bark or similar bulky organic matter. Avoid fresh manure, but pre-packed, well-rotted manure from garden centres is fine, as is well-rotted manure obtained from stables and farmers. In heavy clay soils it is also worth digging in some sharp sand or grit to improve drainage.

Adding a general fertilizer such as blood, fish and bone, or even a controlled-release fertilizer, will help get the bulbs off to the best possible start. You can also add fertilizer when planting, placing it in the hole – provided it is well mixed with the soil at the bottom of the hole – and mixing it in with the soil and organic matter used to refill the hole.

Planting step-by-step

Make sure the planting hole is at least twice the diameter of the bulb. The depth will depend on the species being planted and specific details are given in the plant directory. As a general guide:

- large bulbs – plant with twice their height of soil above them, for example, a 5cm (2in) high bulb should be planted in a 15cm (6in) deep hole
- smaller bulbs – planted with one to one-and-a-half times their height of soil above them
- soil types – on sandy soils you can plant slightly deeper; on clay soils, especially those that do not drain very well, you may need to plant more shallow.

Trowels and bulb planters are the most useful tools for planting bulbs

WHAT TOOLS WILL I NEED?

The type of tool you use will depend on the type of bulb and where you intend to plant.

Trowel Most bulbs can be planted using a garden trowel, especially where you are digging individual planting holes for each one.

Planter A bulb planter can also be used in these situations or where you want to plant a large number of bulbs. Although easy to use in most soils, they can be difficult to use when planting in heavy clay soil.

Spade When planting a large number of bulbs in large groups or when planting in grass use a garden spade to dig out a trench of the right depth.

Add a general fertilizer to the soil before forking it over [A]. Dig a hole of the appropriate size (see page 11) [B]. It often pays to put a 5–10cm (2–4in) layer of sharp sand in the base of the hole if the soil is heavy, especially where the plant needs really good drainage, and plant the bulbs on top of this.

Plant the bulb the right way up (i.e. with the basal plate at the bottom), ensuring its base is in good contact with the soil [C]. Cover the bulb with the excavated soil, having first added extra organic material and sharp sand, if needed. Firm the soil in place but not so much that it becomes compacted [D]. There is not usually any need to water in bulbs after planting.

A

B

C

D

TIP

It often pays to label where the bulbs are planted to prevent you digging them up later by mistake! For the same reason, if you are planting up a bed or entire garden, it is a good idea to plant the bulbs last of all – it is far easier to work bulbs in around perennials and shrubs, for example, than the other way round.

A

B

C

D

E

Naturalizing

Some bulb species grow well and look very natural when planted in lawns, around trees or in rougher grass areas. The best way to plant bulbs in the lawn or naturalize them in rougher grass is to cut the turf into an 'H' shape and peel back the resulting flaps [A]. Prepare the soil [B] and plant as described above [C]. Replace the turf flaps when you have finished planting [D] and lightly firm them down [E]. Use the same method for planting around trees if there is lawn around the base, but ensure you plant away from any large structural roots.

BULBS FOR NATURALIZING

LAWN
Camassia quamash, Chionodoxa, Colchicum, Crocus, Eranthis, *Galanthus nivalis*, Muscari, Narcissus, Paradisea, Puschkinia, *Tulipa praestans, T. praestans*

ROUGH GRASS
Anthericum, Crocus, Hyacinthoides, *Leucojum aestivum* and *L. vernum*, Narcissus

AROUND TREES
Anemone blanda, Arisarum, *Camassia quamash*, Cyclamen, Erythronium, Galanthus, Hyacinthoides, Narcissus, Puschkinia, Trillium, *Tulipa praestans*

Growing in Pots

Where garden space is at a premium or you want seasonal displays near to the house, planting in containers – even hanging baskets – is a great way to display bulbs.

Most bulbs are perfectly happy in containers, providing you take care of the subsequent watering and feeding they will need. In fact, some species, such as Agapanthus and Alstroemeria, grow better in containers where the restricted root run encourages flowering. Half-hardy or tender bulbs, such as Eucomis, Hedychium and Watsonia, are often grown in pots because it makes overwintering them indoors that much easier.

Those that need good drainage – for example, Chlidanthus and Freesia – are certainly good choices for pot culture in gardens where the soil is heavy and prone to waterlogging. And those with small flowers that can look lost in beds and borders become treasures of absolute beauty when viewed close up in a pot – Puschkinia and Rhodohypoxis are two such plants.

Planting in a container

When planting up bulbs in a bowl or container, make sure there are plenty of drainage holes in the base of the container and then add 2.5cm (1in) of grit, gravel or similar to aid drainage. Then fill the container with either loam-free or loam-based John Innes compost.

> **BULBS FOR CONTAINERS**
>
> **SPRING**
> Anemone blanda, Chionodoxa, Crocus, *Cyclamen repandum*, Erythronium, Fritillaria, Hippeastrum, Hyacinthus, Iris, Lachenalia, Leucojum, Muscari, Narcissus, Scilla, Tecophilaea, Tulipa, Veltheimia
>
> **SUMMER**
> Achimenes, Agapanthus, Alstroemeria, *Anemone coronaria*, Begonia, Canna, Chlidanthus, Crocosmia, *Cyclamen purpurascens*, Cyrtanthus, Eucharis, Eucomis, Freesia, Haemanthus, Hedychium, Homeria, Hymenocallis, Ixia, Lilium, Polianthes, Ranunculus, Rhodohypoxis, Scadoxus, Tigridia, Tritonia, Watsonia
>
> **AUTUMN**
> Achimenes, Agapanthus, Amaryllis, Colchicum, Crocus, *Cyclamen cilicium*, *C. hederifolium*, Hedychium, Nerine, Polianthes, Schizostylis, Sternbergia, Zephyranthes
>
> **WINTER**
> Chionodoxa, Crocus, *Cyclamen coum*, Eranthis, Galanthus, Hippeastrum, Iris, Lachenalia, Veltheimia

Layered planting

Container planting also gives you the scope to produce really dramatic displays over several months as you can plant in layers of different species at different depths. For instance, planting daffodils, followed by tulips and then crocuses can provide displays for up to five months. For the most dramatic displays, plant the bulbs close together, leaving about 2.5cm (1in) or so between each one in a layer.

After adding 2.5cm (1in) of drainage material followed by double that amount of compost, arrange the tulip bulbs in the container, ensuring there is a gap of 2.5cm (1in) or so between each bulb [A]. Carefully cover the daffodils with a 5–8cm (2–3in) layer of compost [B] and lightly firm it down between the bulbs.

Add the tulip bulbs using the same method, spacing them evenly apart [C] and again cover them with a 5–8cm (2–3in) layer of lightly firmed compost [D]. Then add a layer of crocus corms [E] for the final layer. Finally, fill the container to within 2.5cm (1in) of the rim with compost [F], lightly firming as you go. The resultant display will be breathtaking.

General Care

The good news is that most bulb species are extremely easy to grow and look after, and with just a little extra care and attention they will reward you with fabulous displays year after year.

Feeding

There are no hard and fast rules for feeding bulbs. In fact, a few bulb species do not respond that well to feeding. However, to ensure quality displays year after year, for most bulbs you will need to provide some extra nutrients both for the current year's display and to feed the storage organ for displays in future years.

It is always a good idea to add a slow-acting fertilizer to the soil at planting time (see page 11) – blood, fish and bone being one of the best choices or, if you prefer, a controlled-release fertilizer (see box). It is important not to overfeed with high nitrogen fertilizers or the leaves may become soft, making them more susceptible to extremes of temperatures, as well as pest and disease problems. Balanced or high potash fertilizers give much better results. Always apply the amount recommended on the container – no more and no less!

Applying a liquid fertilizer is often the easiest method of feeding

When to feed

The critical feeding time for bulbs is from the onset of flowering to when the leaves start to turn yellow. Feeding the plants during this time will help to ensure a profuse flush of flowers the following year because the bulb has to build up its strength, and some have to produce the coming year's flower buds. Feeding at this time is best done using a liquid fertilizer watered onto the soil and over the foliage. This can be done with either a watering can or through a hose attachment.

Container and naturalized bulbs

Plants growing in containers will definitely need feeding and this is again best achieved with regular liquid feeds or adding a controlled-release fertilizer at planting time.

> **CONTROLLED-RELEASE FERTILIZER**
>
> Controlled-release fertilizers only release their nutrients when the soil or compost is warm and moist – that is, the conditions necessary for the plants to grow. If the soil or compost is dry and cold, conditions that do not encourage plant growth, then the nutrients remain locked in. This means that nutrient release only happens when the plant needs them, and also helps ensure no under- or overfeeding, and no leaching of the nutrients out of the soil or compost.

Bulbs that are naturalized in grass often fail to flower if they are not fed at least once when in growth. You can either do this with a standard granular or liquid feed or, if you are feeding the lawn, some of the nutrients will be used by the bulbs. Make sure you use a straight fertilizer and not a feed and weed, as the weedkiller part will also kill off the bulbs!

Watering

Watering dormant bulbs is a complete waste of time and, in some cases, can be very harmful as some from hot climates need a dry dormant period.

Spring-flowering bulbs

Usually there is little need to water spring-flowering bulbs up to flowering, unless the winter or spring are exceptionally dry. However, watering may be needed after flowering to keep the leaves green for as long as possible so that they can continue to feed the bulb for the following year's display.

Keep container bulbs moist but never too wet

Summer-flowering bulbs

Summer-flowering bulbs, on the other hand, may need regular watering when in growth during dry and warm periods to prevent the plants drying out. When watering plants in the ground it is important to give good long soaks rather than the 'little and often' approach as the water has to be able to get down to the roots.

Container bulbs

Plants growing in pots and containers should be checked regularly. Generally, the aim should be to keep the compost moist but not too wet or waterlogged.

Staking

Few bulb species require staking, but it is a good idea to give some of the taller types a bit of support, especially in windy or exposed gardens.

Gladioli, large-flowered dahlias and large-flowered begonias, for example, will all benefit from tying their flowering stems to bamboo canes or similar supports.

Plants that produce large clumps are often best supported by inserting a triangle of supports around the

Support plants such as cannas

edge of the plant and then using loops of string around all three supports, rather than tying the stem directly to the support. Some forced bulbs may produce soft, leggy growth in warm temperatures and their stems can be tied to small split canes.

After Flowering

After flowering, many gardeners think that the bulb has done its job and that no further care or attention is needed. The truth is that the after-flowering period is one of the most important in the bulb's lifecycle.

Carefully deadhead tulips

Deadheading

Most bulb species will benefit from deadheading once the flowers start to fade or else the plant will put its energy into producing seeds at the expense of building up the bulb's strength and food reserves and the following year's flower buds. This can result in little or no flowers the following year. The faded flowers, plus any developing seed capsule below, should be removed with a sharp knife, pair of scissors, secateurs or finger and thumb – do not tug them off. Leave the stems in place, unless otherwise recommended in the plant directory, as these will also help feed the bulb.

Foliage

Sadly, the foliage of many bulbs can look unsightly after flowering and there is always a temptation to remove the leaves or, with daffodils, tie the foliage in neat knots. Resist this at all costs. The foliage is essential for

It may look neat, but tying up daffodils will affect next year's flowering

feeding the bulb to produce the flower buds for the following year; no foliage means no flowers! Once the foliage is yellow or brown it can be carefully removed. If you have to remove the foliage earlier, then wait at least six to eight weeks after flowering as most of the leaves' work will have been done by then.

One way round the problem of the unsightly foliage is to plant other suitable plants around the bulbs to help mask the foliage.

Winter Protection & Storage

The truly hardy bulb species – such as Crocus, Cyclamen, Galanthus and Narcissus – are normally kept in their flowering positions from year to year and they rarely come to any harm. Others may need to be put into storage over the winter or summer months. Storage requirements vary from genus to genus and you will find any specific instructions in the plant directory section.

Tulips – store or leave in the ground?

Although tulips are hardy, some gardeners prefer to lift the bulbs as soon as the foliage has faded after flowering and store them in a dry place, ready to plant again the following autumn. This is because they need a fairly warm, dry rest period in summer while dormant. However, the bulbs can deteriorate rapidly in storage if not given the right conditions, so other gardeners prefer to keep them in the ground all year. If you want to keep yours in the ground, don't plant them in areas where you will be growing plants that need plenty of watering.

Overwintering tender and semi-hardy bulbs

Tender species, such as those that are permanently grown indoors, or those that are planted out for the summer, such as begonias, should always be lifted in the autumn and protected under cover. Keep them cool, but frost free during the winter months. Those with fleshy roots, such as Dahlia and Canna, should be stored in just moist compost or similar material to prevent them drying out.

Yet others are borderline cases and you can take the risk of leaving them outside during the winter if you live in mild regions and your soil is well drained; these include Canna, Dahlia and Gladioli. To help ensure successful overwintering of these outside you should mulch the soil with around 10cm (4in) of compost, straw or similar insulating material.

Protect plants over winter with a good layer of mulch

TIP

One drawback of leaving semi-hardy plants outside for the winter – beside the fact they may die – is that they tend to come into growth quite late in the spring and, as a result, will either flower very late in the year or, sometimes, not at all.

Indoor Displays

While some tender bulb species have to be grown permanently indoors – or only put outside during warm, settled weather in summer – many hardy types can also be used for indoor displays.

Any hardy garden bulb that is suitable for growing in a container outdoors can be used for indoor displays. The planted containers should be left outside until the flower buds appear and then brought indoors. Make sure you position the containers in good light and in a cool room; high temperatures can cause leggy growth and poor flowers. After flowering the containers can be put outside again but the plants may need a period of hardening off first to get used to outdoor conditions.

Forcing bulbs

Some spring-flowering bulbs can be 'forced' so that they flower indoors earlier than they would if grown outside. The bulbs should be planted in containers with good drainage using either a good potting compost or bulb fibre, however the former is best if you intend to plant the bulbs in the garden afterwards. Put a layer of compost in the container and place the bulbs on this close together, but not so close that they touch each other or the side of the container [A]. Plant so that once the container has been filled to within 1cm (½in) of the rim the tips of the bulbs just poke out. Continue to fill, working compost in between the bulbs [B]. When finished [C], water so that the planting medium is moist.

A

B

Now place the container in a cold but frost-free place in the dark; 4°C (40°F) is the ideal temperature for most bulb species. This can be achieved by plunging the container in a shallow trench or standing it somewhere safe in the garden and then covering with around 10cm (4in) of compost, sand, ashes or straw. An alternative method is to place the container in a thick black plastic bag, or put it in a light-proof box and stand it in a garage, shed or cellar.

C

The forcing period can take anything up to 15 weeks, so check regularly for signs of growth. When the shoots are 2.5–5cm (1–2in) long, they can be brought into a light, but not bright, cool room – around 10°C (50°F) – for a few weeks until the flower buds can be seen, then moved to their flowering position. Forced bulbs should not be used for forcing the following year but can be planted in the garden after hardening off.

This display shows off container bulbs in all their glory

Propagation

There are various methods by which bulbs can be propagated, depending to a large extend on the type of planting material you are dealing with.

Division

Bulbs Most true bulbs produce one or more offsets from their basal plate; large offsets are referred to as daughter bulbs, whereas smaller ones are called bulblets. Often the bulbs produce so many offsets the clumps become crowded and flowering is affected as a result.

To divide, carefully lift them at the time recommended in the plant directory. You can then either separate the large clumps into smaller ones or separate all the bulbs and their bulblets and replant them. Small bulblets can take a couple of years to reach flowering size.

Remove bulb offsets and replant

Corms Most corms also produce offsets. As the old corm starts to die a new one is produced above it, together with a number of smaller corms or cormlets. The clumps of corms can be separated into smaller clumps, or you can remove the cormlets for planting up individually. As with bulblets, cormlets can take two to three years before they start flowering.

Tubers Tubers grow larger each year but do not produce offsets, nor do they break up into smaller plants. To divide, carefully dig them up and with a sharp knife cut the tuber into two or more pieces. Each piece must have at least one growing point. It is a good idea to treat the cut surfaces with sulphur powder before re-planting to prevent rotting. The one exception is Cyclamen as the tubers do not respond well to being lifted and divided, so buy new tubers if you want more plants.

Cut Canna tubers with a sharp knife

Rhizomes These are similar to tubers and should also be carefully lifted and cut into sections, ensuring each section has at least one growing point. Old and exhausted sections, and those without growing points, should be discarded. As with tubers, treat cut surfaces with sulphur powder.

Tuberous roots These can also be divided into sections, but wait until the growing points at the top of the roots have just started into growth and are easily visible. Cut off each individual root with a sharp knife, ensuring each has a growing point at the top and a small section of the previous year's stem.

Cuttings

Probably the best way of propagating begonias and dahlias is to take cuttings from young shoots in spring. This has the added advantage that the new plants produced from the cuttings have extra vigour and produce more and better blooms.

Do not take cuttings from plants already growing outside. Instead, begin the process with dormant tubers and encourage them to shoot in controlled conditions. The tubers should be planted in moist compost – begonias should be settled onto the compost – and put in a propagator or other warm place at a temperature of 10–12°C (50–54°F).

Once the shoots that are formed are 7.5–10cm (3–4in) long they should be carefully removed at their base with a sharp knife. Remove the leaves from the lower half of the cutting, dip the base in hormone rooting powder and insert into pots of 50:50 peat or coir and sharp sand or vermiculite. Cover the pots with a polythene bag or place them in a propagator. They will need a temperature of around 12–15°C (54–60°F) and they should root within

Using a sharp knife, remove shoots at their base from the tuber

Put the cuttings around the edge of a small pot filled with compost

two to three weeks when they can be transplanted individually into 9cm (3½in) pots of potting compost.

Once the plants are big enough and have developed a good root system they can be planted outside after hardening off in a cold frame or similar place for ten to 14 days, following the last frosts.

Scaling

Lilies are easily propagated using individual scales. Lift and clean a mature bulb in late summer. Discard any damaged outer scales and carefully snap off a few scales from the bulb as close as possible to the base [A]. Mix slightly damp peat and perlite in 50:50 proportions [B]. Put the mixture in a plastic bag and place the lily scales inside [C]. Shake the bag and fill with air before sealing and labelling [D]. Place in a warm (21°C/70°F), dark place for six weeks. Some lilies, such as *Lilium martagon*, need a further six weeks at 5°C (40°F).

When bulblets appear at the base of the scales, pot them up individually, covered with their own depth of compost. Do not remove the scale if it has roots coming from the base.

Scoring & Scooping

Chionodoxa (Glory of the snow), Crocus, Gladiolus, Hyacinthus, Narcissus (daffodil) and Tulipa can be propagated by a method called scoring, which encourages the bulbs to make young bulblets at their base.

In autumn, start by making two cuts to a depth of no more than one-third of the height of the bulb through the basal plate to make an X [A]. Place the bulb in a warm, dry environment for at least a day, which will open up the cuts and allow their edges to dry out. Then lightly dust the cut surfaces with sulphur powder, which will prevent any rotting infections damaging the bulb [B].

Place the bulb upside down in a tray filled with sand or vermiculite [C] and put this in a dark place at around

Lilium bulbiferum

LILY BULBILS

Some lilies, such as *Lilium tigrinum*, *L. bulbiferum*, *L. leichtinii* and *L. sargentiae*, produce small bulbs (bulbils) in the leaf axils of the stems. When these are ripe they detach easily and can be pressed into the surface of a pot of compost. Cover with 13mm (½in) of coarse sand or fine grit. Keep the pots frost free over winter, and plant out the following autumn.

A

B

C

D

21°C (70°F); an airing cupboard is an excellent place to do this. Keep the bulb as dry as possible, but do not allow the scale leaves to dry out. You can prevent this by dampening the sand or vermiculite occasionally.

In two to three months the new bulblets will develop on the cut surfaces. When bulblets have been produced, plant the bulb upside down in a pot of John Innes compost so that the bulblets are just below the surface of the compost [D]. Harden off for a week to ten days and put the pot in a frost-free cold frame or similar position.

In spring, the bulblets will grow and produce leaves. At the end of autumn, lift and separate the bulblets and replant them in pots of compost or plant in the garden. Bulblets will reach flowering size in two to three years.

A similar method called scooping involves scooping out the entire basal plate in one movement with a sharp knife or, better still, an old teaspoon with a sharpened edge. The bulb is then treated in the same way as for scoring. This method produces lots more but smaller bulblets that can take three to four years to reach flowering size.

Planting Combinations

Bulbs are a hugely versatile group of plants and should play a vital role in brightening up every garden throughout the year. This is because you can always find something in flower, all year round. Although the spring-flowering species are the most popular, more use should be made of the summer, autumn and even winter-flowering types to ensure your garden has colour and interest in every month. And because there is such a wide spectrum of colours in the world of bulbs, they help bring added life to all displays no matter where they occur – both indoors and outside.

Sadly, bulbs are often seen by gardeners as plants that are just dotted here and there in small numbers to give a bit of extra spring colour; rarely are they planted en masse to provide bold, bright, colourful displays. However, they can also be much more important and more versatile than that.

Planted as part of mixed borders they can play a number of important roles, such as extending the flowering seasons and therefore the period of interest; as weed-suppressing ground cover and used for underplanting other plants; helping to quickly and cheaply fill bare or dull spots or hiding the bare stems of shrubs and climbers; providing height at the back of borders; and adding to the general 'flower power' of the display. Because many bulbs will quite happily grow through other plants you can use them to extend the interest of plants with short flowering periods – something that is essential in small gardens if you are to make the utmost of the limited space.

Luckily, many bulbs flower at times of year when few other plants are providing structure, form and colour, and hence help ensure your garden can be colourful all year round. One major example of this is during winter and early spring when gardens can look as dull as the weather. One classic planting combination for this time of year brings together the red stems of *Cornus alba* 'Sibirica' with the ornamental foliage and flowers of *Helleborus foetidus* and an underplanting of snowdrops

> **TIP**
>
> As most bulbs are upright plants with thin, grassy or sword-like foliage, they always look good when planted in combination with plants with large, rounded leaves such as hostas and ligularias, for instance.

Crocuses look spectacular planted in swathes

Shorter plants can be used to hide the longer, straggly stems of taller plants

TIP

Displays always look more effective if you plant a larger amount of a small number of types and cultivars in a restricted colour range, rather than a small number of a wide range of types and colours. Sticking to displays consisting purely of strong 'hot colours' (reds, yellows, oranges and purples) or pale 'cool colours' (pinks, blues, silver and white) always looks effective and dramatic. For a superb summer combination, why not try the pale silvery pink *Dahlia* 'Pearl of Heemstede' with *Verbena bonariensis* and blue larkspurs (Consolida).

(Galanthus), but any bulb flowering at this time will lift grey spirits. Similarly, during autumn, Colchicum, Crinum, Cyclamen, Dahlia and Nerine can ensure the garden remains bright and colourful either up to or well beyond the first heavy frosts, depending on hardiness.

Planted as part of bedding displays, they can help bring much welcome height to what would otherwise be a very flat, almost two-dimensional planting. Tulips planted among wallflowers and forget-me-nots, and cannas, gladioli, lilies and dahlias planted among summer-flowering bedding displays are just two cases in point.

With global warming, climate change and drier summers becoming more important factors that will affect gardens and gardeners and the trend towards Mediterranean and other 'exotic' planting styles, many bulbs fit in perfectly with such topics and schemes. This is especially true of Allium, Canna, Crinum, Crocosmia, Eucomis, Gladiolus, Hedychium, Nerine, Zantedeschia and Zephyranthes, which can be planted on their own or with palms and hardy bananas, for example.

As patio and container gardening becomes more and more popular, bulbs again play a vital part because there are so many types that are perfectly at home in pots, window boxes, other containers and hanging baskets. Bulbs can either be grown on their own – try them in

layers of different species for a long flowering period (see page 13) – or mixed with shrubs, herbaceous plants and bedding for providing added interest and extending the flowering periods; pop in a few crocus, snowdrops, dwarf daffodils or tulips in spring-flowering pots and hanging baskets. You can even grow bulbs in pots that are then stood on, or sunk into the soil, in bare spots of beds and borders. As the flowers die off, remove the pots and replace with others containing something else in flower – a quick and easy way of ensuring the garden will always look its best.

Where space allows, massed planting will always look colourful and effective. For instance, you cannot beat the ground covering carpet display of winter aconites (Eranthis) with snowdrops and even scillas to blow away the late winter and spring blues, or hardy cyclamen for mouth-watering autumn and winter cheer.

There are bulbs for every occasion, every situation, every month, every garden and every gardener – so why not get planting some today? A number of planting combinations are given throughout the A-Z section of this book to help you decide what to plant and where.

A beautiful combination of tulips among primulas

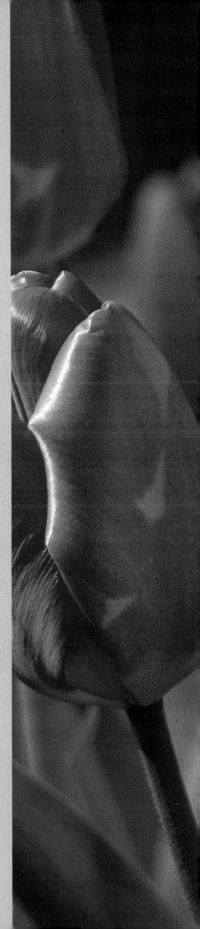
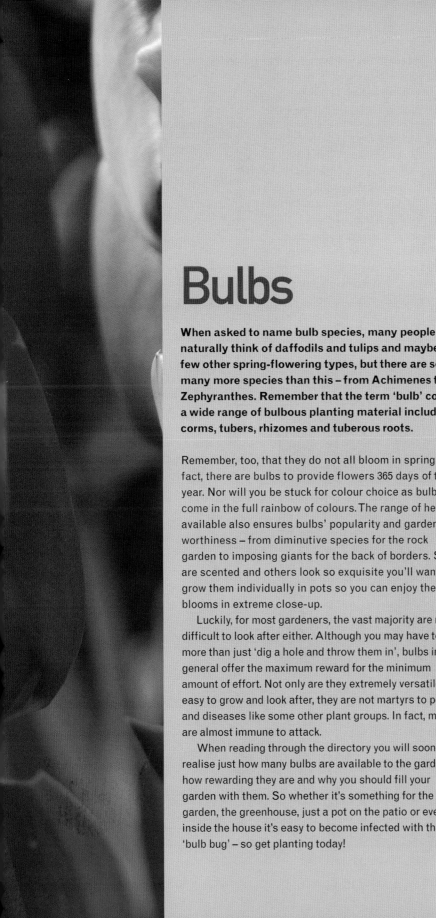

Bulbs

When asked to name bulb species, many people will naturally think of daffodils and tulips and maybe a few other spring-flowering types, but there are so many more species than this – from Achimenes to Zephyranthes. Remember that the term 'bulb' covers a wide range of bulbous planting material including corms, tubers, rhizomes and tuberous roots.

Remember, too, that they do not all bloom in spring – in fact, there are bulbs to provide flowers 365 days of the year. Nor will you be stuck for colour choice as bulbs come in the full rainbow of colours. The range of heights available also ensures bulbs' popularity and garden worthiness – from diminutive species for the rock garden to imposing giants for the back of borders. Some are scented and others look so exquisite you'll want to grow them individually in pots so you can enjoy the blooms in extreme close-up.

Luckily, for most gardeners, the vast majority are not difficult to look after either. Although you may have to do more than just 'dig a hole and throw them in', bulbs in general offer the maximum reward for the minimum amount of effort. Not only are they extremely versatile, easy to grow and look after, they are not martyrs to pests and diseases like some other plant groups. In fact, many are almost immune to attack.

When reading through the directory you will soon realise just how many bulbs are available to the gardener, how rewarding they are and why you should fill your garden with them. So whether it's something for the garden, the greenhouse, just a pot on the patio or even for inside the house it's easy to become infected with the 'bulb bug' – so get planting today!

Achimenes

Hot water plant
RHIZOME
(TUBERCLES)

An attractive indoor plant for the home, conservatory or greenhouse, Achimenes produce masses of flowers on compact plants. Even the shiny, velvety leaves are attractive.

The hot water plant is an easy one to grow and is a beautiful plant for indoors, where you will be rewarded by masses of trumpet-shaped blooms over several months. It gets its common name from the erroneous idea that the tubercles could only be encouraged into growth by dousing with hot water.

The tubercles should be potted up from late winter to early spring in slightly moist compost using six tubercles to a 15cm (6in) pot. Trailing cultivars are best displayed and planted in hanging baskets or pots; plant two tubercles in a 9cm (3½in) pot and transplant into the basket when they have developed a good root system.

Once shoots appear, start watering more liberally. Pinching back the stems of young plants will help to develop a bushier habit.

soil	Loam-free compost is the preferred type of soil in which these plants will flourish
site	Site in a position in bright light, however, keep away from direct sun
planting	When first planting the tubercles, place them 2cm (¾in) deep
general care	Keep compost moist, but allow to dry out once flowering has finished; then cut off dead stems. Feed fortnightly when in growth
pests & diseases	Generally free of problems from pests and diseases, but can suffer attack from aphids and thrips

Achimenes 'Purple King'

As the stems are quite weak, upright cultivars may need staking with split canes to help support the stems and foliage. The plants prefer a humid atmosphere, so mist the foliage daily with tepid water.

When the stems start to die down in autumn, stop watering and feeding, and give the tubercles a winter rest. In winter or spring carefully remove them from the pot, separate them from the compost and pot up in fresh compost. Each plant will have produced several new tubercles during the previous year, so there will be lots more to pot up. The plants require reasonable warmth when growing – 15–18°C (60–65°F). Keep dormant tubercles at a minimum of 5°C (41°F).

	SPRING	SUMMER	AUTUMN	WINTER	height (cm)	spread (cm)	flower colour	
Achimenes 'Ambroise Verschaffelt'	planting	● ● ● ● ●	● ● ●	planting planting	15	30	☐	Trailing habit; flowers are veined purple
A. 'Cattleya'	planting	● ● ● ●	● ●	planting planting	15	30	■	Trailing habit
A. 'Flamingo'	planting	● ● ● ●	● ●	planting planting	30	30	■	Trailing habit
A. 'Paul Arnold'	planting	● ● ● ●	● ●	planting planting	30	30	■	Upright habit
A. 'Peach Blossom'	planting	● ● ● ●	● ●	planting planting	15	30	☐	Trailing habit
A. 'Purple King'	planting	● ● ● ●	● ●	planting planting	20	30	■	Partly trailing habit
A. 'Snow Princess'	planting	● ● ● ●	● ●	planting planting	30	25	☐	Upright habit

planting   ● flowering

Agapanthus
African lily
RHIZOME

The dramatic flowerheads of Agapanthus make it a must for exotic borders and, originating from warm climates, perfect for drought and gravel gardens. Agapanthus is also a top choice for container growing.

Agapanthus praecox

The boom in holidays to destinations such as South Africa and Madeira has increased the popularity of Agapanthus. Gardeners are so smitten with it when they see it growing wild that they can be tempted to bring back plants to grow at home. However, *Agapanthus africanus* is not hardy and needs overwintering in a frost-free place at 5°C (41°F). *A. campanulatus* is hardier and plants can be left outside over winter, but protect the crowns with compost, bark or similar insulating material. The former is evergreen, whereas *A. campanulatus* is deciduous and will lose its leaves during autumn.

The umbels of large, trumpet-shaped flowers can be as much as 20cm (8in) across and make dramatic displays – especially when grown in containers. Plants can take a while to settle down and get into regular flowering mode. Growing plants in containers aids flowering due to the container restricting root growth. *A. africanus* should be grown in containers to make it easier to bring under cover for the winter.

In containers, keep them as potbound as possible to improve flowering. When these or those grown in the garden need dividing, do this in mid-spring, but dividing will reduce flowering in the first few years.

Not only is Agapanthus an excellent plant

A. praecox subsp. maximus 'Albus'

for garden decoration, but the flower stems can be cut and dried for indoor displays and arrangements.

soil	Agapanthus requires well-drained, fertile soil or loam-based compost
site	A position in full sun is needed for these plants to flourish
planting	When first planting the rhizomes, place 10cm (4in) deep, 45–60cm (18–24in) apart
general care	Water during long dry periods and feed with a high potash fertilizer – especially plants in containers – during the summer
pests & diseases	Generally trouble free, although slugs and snails, as well as viruses can affect plants

	SPRING	SUMMER	AUTUMN	WINTER	height (cm)	spread (cm)	flower colour	
Agapanthus africanus	🌱		● ● ●		60	75	■	Evergreen
A. africanus 'Albus'	🌱		● ● ●		60	75	□	Evergreen
A. 'Blue Giant'	🌱		● ● ●		110	90	■	Deciduous
A. campanulatus	🌱		● ● ●		75	100	▨	Deciduous
A. campanulatus 'Isis'	🌱		● ● ●		75	90	■	Deciduous
A. campanulatus subsp. patens	🌱		● ● ●		70	80	□	Deciduous
A. Headbourne Hybrids	🌱		● ● ●		90	60	▨	Deciduous
A. praecox	🌱		● ● ●		90	60	▨	Evergreen

 planting   ● flowering

Allium

Flowering onion
BULB

Alliums are one of the trendiest bulbs to grow at the moment – you only have to notice how many are used in the gardens and displays at flower shows to see that. They are easy to grow and produce glowing displays in the garden.

Not only are alliums colourful and cheery garden plants, they are extremely versatile. There are several types, some suitable for the middle or back of beds and borders, while others, the lower-growing ones, make excellent rockery and edging plants. It is even thought that underplanting roses with alliums can deter pests and diseases.

There are two basic types: those with ball-shaped flowerheads and those with more open clusters of upright or drooping flowers.

The foliage may be large and strap like, making sturdy clumps, or finer and grass like, producing a more delicate appearance. The foliage smells of onions when crushed or bruised. Those plants producing ball-shaped flowers and strappy foliage are best for beds, whereas those with fine foliage and open flowers are best for edging or for growing on rockeries.

Most alliums are perfectly hardy, certainly all those listed here, apart from *Allium*

Allium 'Globemaster'

Allium moly

Allium cristophii

soil	For best results, plant alliums in any fertile, well-drained soil	
site	These plants prefer a sunny position in the garden for them to really flourish	
planting	Cover up to two times the height of the bulb; 15–30cm (6–12in) apart depending on height	
general care	Leave plants undisturbed for several years to improve flowering. Overcrowded clumps can be split once stems die down	
pests & diseases	Alliums can be attacked by pests such as onion fly and diseases such as white rot and rust	

Allium unifolium

giganteum. But some, such as *A. cyaneum* and *A. oreophilum*, can also be grown in pots in a cool greenhouse or alpine house where their flowers can be better appreciated.

Many species are superb cut for indoor decorations, because they last well in water, and the large flowerheads of *A. cristophii* and others can be dried for use in flower arrangements.

Nearly all alliums set seed freely, so unless you want masses of seedlings it is a good idea to cut off the flowerheads once they have faded.

Allium karataviense

	SPRING	SUMMER	AUTUMN	WINTER	height (cm)	spread (cm)	flower colour	
Allium caeruleum	●	●			60	30		Small spherical heads
A. cristophii		● ●			50	30		Ball-shaped flowers
A. cyaneum		● ● ●			25	25		Pendent flowers
A. flavum		● ● ●			30	15		Pendent flowers
A. giganteum	●	●			180	50		Ball-shaped flowers
A. 'Gladiator'		● ●			120	40		Ball-shaped flowers
A. 'Globemaster'	●	●			90	30		Ball-shaped flowers
A. hollandicum 'Purple Sensation'	● ●	●			100	30		Ball-shaped flowers
A. karataviense	●	●			30	50		Ball-shaped flowers
A. moly	●	●			30	30		Upright flowers
A. oreophilum	● ●	●			20	20		Loose heads of bell-shaped flowers
A. sphaerocephalon		● ● ●			90	50		Heads of upright flowers
A. triquetrum	● ●				30	20		Pendent flowers with green stripe. Give plenty of space
A. unifolium	● ● ●				60	30		Rounded heads of bell-shaped flowers

 planting   ● flowering

Alstroemeria

Peruvian lily
TUBEROUS ROOT

This colourful perennial has become more and more popular in recent years, mostly thanks to the breeding of more compact, hardier, longer flowering cultivars in a wider range of colours.

An *Alstroemeria* Ligtu hybrid

The Peruvian lily was often thought of as a garden thug – the creeping roots would take over the garden – and the plants were shy to flower or did not flower for very long. But recent improvements, especially with the introduction of the Princess series, have resulted in more garden-friendly plants that are easy to look after and stay in flower for several months.

Although alstroemerias are perfect border plants, as long as they are given plenty of space, those cultivars that flower over a long time also make perfect container plants, soon filling a decent sized pot. The short cultivars can even be grown in hanging baskets. Container growing not only keeps the roots from spreading too far, but it also improves flowering. Always keep

soil	Requires well-drained, light soil or loam-based compost for best results
site	Performs well if positioned either in full sun or light shade
planting	Plant 10cm (4in) deep, 30cm (12in) apart in the garden or 5cm (2in) deep in 30cm (12in) pots
general care	Protect young plants from bright sunlight and water regularly until established. Deadhead for continuous flowering
pests & diseases	Slugs and snails may attack young shoots. Red spider mite can be a problem for plants under glass

Alstroemeria 'Friendship'

the compost moist and feed fortnightly when in flower to encourage even more flowers.

The open, funnel-shaped flowers are about 5cm (2in) long and produced in loose clusters. Many cultivars produce flowers that are variously marked in contrasting colours adding greatly to their overall attraction to the gardener.

The cut flowers will last for a long time in water, making them a favourite with florists and hence all flower arrangers.

The roots are fleshy but brittle and should be planted as soon as possible, taking care not to damage them. Although the roots should be planted in spring, pot-grown plants can be planted any time from spring to late summer.

Plants are best left alone to increase in size and hence flower profusely, but they can be split and divided in spring, but only when overcrowding makes it essential.

Generally hardy down to -10°C (14°F), the plants should be protected with a thick mulch in autumn especially in cold and exposed areas. Although stems may come through the winter they are best cut down in spring. Plants grown in pots are best overwintered in a light, frost-free place, keeping the compost almost dry. They can then be moved outside after the danger of frosts has passed.

	SPRING	SUMMER	AUTUMN	WINTER	height (cm)	spread (cm)	flower colour	
Alstroemeria 'Apollo'	planting	flowering			90	50		Flowers streaked with dark brown, flushed deep yellow
A. aurea 'Lutea'	planting	flowering			100	60		Flowers have brown specks
A. aurea 'Orange King'	planting	flowering			100	60		Flowers marked with yellow
A. 'Coronet'	planting	flowering			100	50		Flowers marked yellow and red
A. Diana Princess of Wales = 'Stablaco'	planting	flowering	flowering		90	50		Flowers have a pink reverse
A. 'Friendship'	planting	flowering	flowering		90	50		Flowers have a yellow speckled throat
A. Ligtu Hybrids	planting	flowering			60	40		Flowers are variously marked
A. 'Orange Glory'	planting	flowering			90	50		Flowers marked yellow and red
A. 'Princess Ivana'	planting	flowering			30	30		Flowers marked with yellow
A. 'Yellow Friendship'	planting	flowering			90	60		Flowers marked with purple and deep yellow

 planting ⊛ flowering

Amaryllis
Belladonna lily
BULB

Do not confuse this plant with the indoor amaryllis – so popular at Christmas – which are actually cultivars of Hippeastrum. This species is hardier and can be grown outside in warm, sheltered positions.

Although similar in appearance to hippeastrums – with lily-like flowers on robust stems – *Amaryllis belladonna* produces smaller, fragrant, trumpet-shaped flowers up to 10cm (4in) long in clusters of 6 to 12. Growing up to 80cm (31in) tall and 45cm (18in) wide, they are excellent for cutting and indoor decoration.

The long, strap-like foliage appears following the flowers in autumn and lasts through winter and into the following summer. This makes the plant susceptible to cold and frost damage, so it is important to mulch the plants in autumn and even

soil	Good, well-drained soil or loam-based compost is ideal for these plants
site	A warm, sheltered site in full sun is essential for Amaryllis to flourish
planting	Plant with the tip of the bulb level with the soil or compost surface; 30cm (12in) apart
general care	Bulbs must receive direct sunlight or they will not flower. Allow leaves and flowers to die back naturally before removing
pests & diseases	Amaryllis can be troubled by attack from slugs, snails, narcissus fly and eelworm, as well as succumbing to bulb rot

Amaryllis belladonna

protect with a cloche or similar covering during winter.

The belladonna lily is not reliably hardy where temperatures regularly fall below -5°C (23°F), in which case plants are best grown as container plants indoors. Place them in good light but out of strong, direct sunlight to avoid the flowers bleaching and to extend their life. Plant in late summer in mild regions only. Otherwise, plant in spring.

It is important to keep the foliage of pot-grown plants growing for as long as possible, and feeding monthly when in leaf with a liquid feed will help build up the bulb for flowering in the following year. Reduce watering as soon as the foliage begins to fade and stop watering altogether when dormant until growth resumes.

Amaryllis prefer to be crowded or potbound so only move them or repot when absolutely necessary during dormancy. Offsets can be removed and potted up separately at the same time.

There is only one species, but there are half a dozen named cultivars with flowers in varying shades of pink and white; however, you may need a specialist supplier for these.

Anemone
Windflower
TUBER *or* RHIZOME

These colourful, generally spring-flowering plants are fairly easy to grow and very versatile, being suitable for naturalizing in grass, producing large drifts under trees, bringing colour to rockeries, beds and borders or even used as a cut flower.

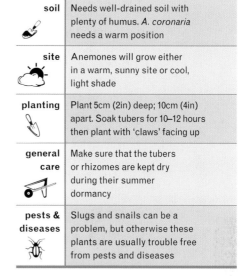
A. coronaria De Caen Group

The plants featured here, as opposed to the herbaceous anemones, can be divided into two groups: those for cool, semi-shaded positions and those that need a hot, dry place.

The first group includes *Anemone apennina* and *A. nemorosa*, the wood anemone, both of which are grown from a rhizome. They grow in full sun but prefer dappled shade or shade during part of the day and are ideal for cool borders, rock gardens and woodland gardens.

A. blanda and *A. coronaria* make up the second group and need full sun and dry conditions, especially when dormant. As well as suitable for growing in the garden they

soil	Needs well-drained soil with plenty of humus. *A. coronaria* needs a warm position
site	Anemones will grow either in a warm, sunny site or cool, light shade
planting	Plant 5cm (2in) deep; 10cm (4in) apart. Soak tubers for 10–12 hours then plant with 'claws' facing up
general care	Make sure that the tubers or rhizomes are kept dry during their summer dormancy
pests & diseases	Slugs and snails can be a problem, but otherwise these plants are usually trouble free from pests and diseases

make excellent pot plants. *A. blanda* is a perfect choice for growing in a dry woodland or for producing large, colourful drifts under trees. They are grown from tubers.

A. coronaria is the florist anemone, which is popular as a cut flower. The De Caen Group is the most commonly grown producing single, cup-shaped flowers in a range of strong colours. The Saint Bridgid Group is similar but the flowers are semi-double or double. Plants can be brought into flower throughout the year; plant in succession in early to mid-autumn for flowers in spring, or spring for flowers in summer and early autumn. Grow at a minimum temperature of 10°C (50°F).

Anemone blanda

	SPRING	SUMMER	AUTUMN	WINTER	height (cm)	spread (cm)	flower colour	
Anemone apennina	● ●		🌱 🌱		15	30		Flowers often flushed pink. Leaves often flushed
A. blanda	● ●		🌱 🌱	●	20	30		Grow with snowdrops (Galanthus) and winter aconites (Eranthis)
A. blanda 'Blue Shades'	● ●		🌱 🌱	●	20	30		Looks good under silver birch (Betula pendula)
A. blanda 'Pink Star'	● ●		🌱 🌱	●	20	30		Looks good with grey-leaved plants
A. blanda 'White Splendour'	● ●		🌱 🌱	●	20	30		Looks good with dogwoods (Cornus)
A. coronaria De Caen Group 'Die Braut'	🌱● 🌱● 🌱	● ● ●	🌱● 🌱●		60	20		Sometimes sold as 'The Bride'
A. coronaria De Caen Group 'Mr Fokker'	🌱● 🌱● 🌱	🌱● 🌱● 🌱	🌱● 🌱● 🌱		60	20		Single flowers
A. coronaria St Bridgid Group 'The Admiral'	🌱● 🌱● 🌱	🌱● 🌱● 🌱	🌱● 🌱● 🌱		60	20		Double flowers
A. nemorosa	● ●		🌱 🌱		15	30		Named cultivars are also available

 planting ● flowering

Anthericum
St Bernard's lily
TUBEROUS ROOT

Although this plant has been grown in gardens for hundreds of years, it has never been particularly popular. This is a shame, as the plant's tall spikes of starry flowers look fantastic in mixed or herbaceous borders.

One of the reasons for its lack of popularity could be that it only starts to flower in the second year after planting. But once established, it produces good sized clumps that have masses of white flowers with yellow stamens on tall stems; those of *Anthericum ramosum* are heavily branched. This makes the plant's stately growth invaluable in herbaceous borders, large rockeries or even naturalizing in grass or adorning lightly shaded woods. Anthericum is also suitable for growing in pots, providing

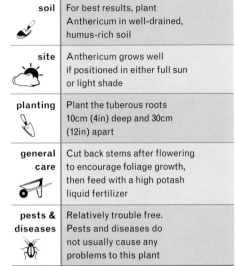

soil	For best results, plant Anthericum in well-drained, humus-rich soil
site	Anthericum grows well if positioned in either full sun or light shade
planting	Plant the tuberous roots 10cm (4in) deep and 30cm (12in) apart
general care	Cut back stems after flowering to encourage foliage growth, then feed with a high potash liquid fertilizer
pests & diseases	Relatively trouble free. Pests and diseases do not usually cause any problems to this plant

Anthericum liliago

they are quite deep. The flowers also last for a long time when cut for indoors.

The grey-green, grass-like foliage is light and open, and does not form dense clumps, which adds to its overall attraction. Always allow the foliage to die down naturally in the autumn.

The plants hate root disturbance, so only lift and divide when absolutely necessary, and certainly not more than every five years. Divided plants often take a year before they flower. It is often better to propagate plants in situ, carefully removing outer sections of root without lifting the plants.

Both species of Anthericum are hardy to -10°C (14°F), and a cold winter actually improves the flowering of *A. liliago*. But a mulch will help during periods of low temperatures when snow cover does not accompany them.

	SPRING	SUMMER	AUTUMN	WINTER	height (cm)	spread (cm)	flower colour	
Anthericum liliago	🌱	● ● ●			75	30	☐	Prominent yellow centre
A. liliago var. *major*	🌱	● ● ●			90	30	☐	Larger flowers than *A. liliago*
A. ramosum	🌱	● ● ●			90	30	☐	Smaller flowers than *A. liliago*

🌱 planting   ● flowering

Arisaema
TUBER

These curiously attractive plants are increasing in popularity and are the perfect choice for very moist soil when you are looking for that unusual talking point to impress friends and neighbours.

The 'flowers' of arisaemas consist of an ornamental leaf-like, tubular hood, called a spathe, surrounding a prominent stalk called a spadix. The flowers are produced in summer before the leaves unfurl. The tiny true flowers are formed around the base of the spadix and turn into orange-red berries after the spathe dies. The berries are poisonous and can also cause skin irritation.

soil	Needs well-drained but moisture-retentive soil enriched with humus
site	These plants grow well if positioned in both the sun or partial shade
planting	Plant Arisaema tubers 15cm (6in) deep and 15cm (6in) apart
general care	Protect the tubers during prolonged freezing periods in winter with a mulch of compost, bark or similar material
pests & diseases	These plants are usually trouble free from pests and diseases, although slugs may attack them

Arisaema griffithii

Arisaemas are grown for their attractive spathes, which are variously striped and marked depending on the species grown. The petioles and leaves are often beautifully marked too, adding to the overall attraction.

Apart from *Arisaema triphyllum*, which is hardier, the other species are usually best planted in autumn in containers of loam-based compost with added extra peat or peat substitute. These can then be overwintered in a cold greenhouse, coldframe or the pot plunged in the soil for frost protection. After flowering the plants can be planted out in the garden in moist border soil or woodland. Alternatively, plant directly in their flowering position in the garden in spring, but be prepared to give protection in winter.

Plants can be propagated by removing offsets from mature plants in late autumn.

	SPRING	SUMMER	AUTUMN	WINTER	height (cm)	spread (cm)	flower colour	
Arisaema candidissimum		● ●			40	20		Rose-scented flowers with pale pink stripes
A. flavum		●			45	25		Flowers purple inside
A. griffithii		● ●			60	45		Flowers are heavily veined
A. triphyllum	●	●			40	30		Flowers often lined with purple

 planting ● flowering

Arisarum

Mouse plant
TUBER

This curious rather than beautiful plant, *Arisarum proboscideum*, is commonly called the mouse plant because of the tail-like tip of the plump flowers that resembles the tail and body of a mouse.

Arisarum proboscideum

Arisarum proboscideum

Arisarum is an unusual plant that provides ideal ground cover in shady positions, including woodland conditions, since the foliage forms dense mats. It can also be grown on moisture retentive rock gardens or in pots or containers. The latter is a good way to grow this plant since children especially can view the flowers close up and enjoy the detail.

The curious flowers appear among the foliage and consist of a small, purplish-brown and white spathe which extends into a 15cm (6in) long tip – the tail of the mouse. Flowers will fade to

soil	Requires well-drained, but moisture retentive, humus-rich soil
site	Needs to be positioned in light or partial shade for best results
planting	Plant Arisarum tubers 15cm (6in) deep and 10cm (4in) apart
general care	Mulch plants with compost, composted bark or leafmould in the spring to help keep humus levels high
pests & diseases	Relatively trouble free. Pests and diseases do not usually cause any problems to this plant

a whitish-blue. The glossy, arrow-shaped foliage grows up to 10cm (4in) long. Plants generally tend to spread to about 20cm (8in).

Plant in the late summer to mid-autumn for flowering in mid- to late spring. In a greenhouse or conservatory, mouse plants should be grown in gritty, humus-rich, loamless potting compost. For best results, position them not in direct sunlight but filtered light if possible. Planting arisarums behind larger plants in the greenhouse or conservatory is an easy solution of filtering direct sunlight away from them.

Outside, partial shade is required for best results, along with humus-rich, moist soil. Although arisarums can tolerate low temperatures, it pays to mulch the plants in winter when extended freezing conditions are expected.

Plants are easy to propagate by dividing overcrowded clumps or removing offset tubers in autumn. Arisarums are also trouble free from pests and diseases, which makes them easy plants to cultivate and maintain.

Arisarum proboscideum

Arum

Cuckoo pint, Jack-in-the-pulpit *or* Lords-and-ladies

TUBER

Large showy spathes, often attractive mottled foliage and colourful berries mean that arums provide interest in the garden for several months. They bear colourful leaf-like spathes up to 40cm (16in) long surrounding a prominent stalk-like spadix usually in spring.

Arum creticum

Arum pictum, however, produces its spathes in the autumn. The true flowers are tiny and produced around the base of the spadix. These give rise to bright red berries in autumn after the foliage and spathes die down.

The large, arrowhead-like leaves up to 35cm (14in) long are usually produced in autumn and winter – although those of the British native *A. maculatum* are formed in spring, helping to extend the period of interest. Nearly all species have colourful markings, those of 'Marmoratum' are so gorgeously marbled that this plant is usually grown mainly for its leaves – the flowers being an added bonus!

Plants can be grown in a variety of positions depending on which part of the world they come from. *A. creticum* is a Mediterranean plant for rock gardens; *A. italicum* is another Mediterranean species but best suited for woodland gardens and shrub beds; *A. maculatum* is suitable for shaded areas and woodland gardens; and *A. pictum* is another Mediterranean resident for the rockery.

Unfortunately, the spathes of most arums (except *A. creticum*) have an unpleasant odour of decay, which is used to attract pollinating insects; the berries are poisonous and the sap and juice of the berries can cause skin irritation.

Plants can be propagated by dividing after flowering, but wear gloves to protect your skin from the sap.

soil	Arums require a well-drained, humus-rich soil for best results
site	Needs to be positioned in light or partial shade for plants to flourish
planting	Plant the tubers 10–12.5cm (4–5in) deep and roughly 20cm (8in) apart
general care	Mulch with compost, composted bark or leafmould in summer and ensure the soil is moist during winter and spring
pests & diseases	Relatively trouble free. Pests and diseases do not usually cause any problems to this plant

Arum pictum

	SPRING	SUMMER	AUTUMN	WINTER	height (cm)	spread (cm)	flower colour	
Arum creticum	flowering	flowering / planting	planting		40	25		Flowers are sweetly scented
A. italicum subsp. *italicum* 'Marmoratum'		flowering / planting	planting		30	40		Foliage with pale veins and grey-green mottling
A. maculatum	flowering	flowering / planting	planting		30	30		Maroon blotched foliage. Orange-red berries
A. pictum		planting	flowering		30	25		Dark green foliage with fine, cream veins

planting   flowering

Asarum
Wild ginger
RHIZOME

If you are looking for a ground cover plant for growing in a shady position in the garden, then wild gingers are an excellent choice. They produce mats of low-growing, glossy green foliage.

The foliage of *Asarum caudatum*, *A. europaeum*, *A. pulchellum* and *A. splendens* is evergreen; *A. canadense* is deciduous. They get their common name from the leaves, which have a gingery or peppery scent and can be up to 15cm (6in) long. Wild gingers look particularly good in moist, woodland situations or cool rockeries in the shade.

soil	For best results, plant Asarum in any moist, but humus-rich soil
site	Requires a position in partial shade for wild ginger to really flourish
planting	Plant asarums 15cm (6in) deep and roughly 30cm (12in) apart
general care	Mulch the plants in the summer with compost, composted bark or leafmould to top up the soil's natural humus levels
pests & diseases	These plants are usually trouble free from pests and diseases, although slugs and snails may attack them

Asarum europaeum

Asarum pulchellum

Although most bulbs are grown for their flowers, those of the asarums are small and fairly insignificant and produced at ground level under the leaves, so you have to look to find them. Curious, rather than attractive, the urn-shaped flowers produce seeds that are interestingly distributed by ants.

Asarums are mainly woodland plants in the wild and are grown best in moist, humus-rich soil. *A. caudatum* and *A. europaeum* are reasonably drought resistant, but benefit from mulching in summer to help maintain soil moisture levels. If planted in open positions you may need to water in hot, dry summers to keep the plants growing well.

Plants are propagated by dividing established clumps in spring.

	SPRING	SUMMER	AUTUMN	WINTER	height (cm)	spread (cm)	flower colour	
Asarum canadense	● ● ●		🖌 🖌		15	25		Green foliage
A. caudatum	● ● ●		🖌 🖌		10	40		Green foliage
A. europaeum	● ● ●		🖌 🖌		10	50		Green foliage sometimes with silver markings
A. pulchellum	● ● ●		🖌 🖌		20	50		Dark green foliage with pewter markings
A. splendens	● ● ●		🖌 🖌		15	25		Dark green foliage with grey/silver mottled markings

🖌 *planting*　　● *flowering*

Asphodeline

Jacob's rod *or*
Yellow asphodel
TUBEROUS ROOT

Tall, graceful spires of yellow starry flowers make Asphodeline a superb choice for herbaceous borders and mixed beds. The most popular species is *Asphodeline lutea*.

A. lutea produces tufts of grey-green, grassy foliage above which the tall, dense spikes of numerous, fragrant flowers up to 3cm (1¼in) across appear. *A. liburnica* is shorter, more slender and refined, producing yellow flowers that are sometimes striped with green.

Although the roots help the plants withstand dry conditions, it pays to water the plants during prolonged drought conditions. A sunny position is preferred, such as in an open border or on a dry, sunny bank, but they will tolerate light, dappled shade.

The roots can be planted in spring or autumn, but autumn planting should be followed by mulching or similar protection if a severe winter is expected.

Plants can be propagated by carefully dividing plants in autumn or spring or by taking softwood cuttings.

soil	For best results, plant Asphodeline in any free draining, fertile soil
site	Asphodeline prefers a sunny position in the garden for it to really thrive
planting	Plant these tuberous roots 10cm (4in) deep and 23cm (9in) apart
general care	Plants do not like a rich soil, so take care not to overfeed or use manure when planting
pests & diseases	May be troubled by slugs, snails and aphids. Apart from these pests, relatively trouble free

Watch out for slugs, snails and aphids, although these are rarely huge problems for asphodelines. There is quite a bit of confusion over naming and some species, especially *A. lutea*, are often classified as Asphodelus (see page 38), so ask a specialist garden centre for advice if there is any doubt.

Asphodeline lutea

Asphodeline lutea

	SPRING	SUMMER	AUTUMN	WINTER	height (cm)	spread (cm)	flower colour	
Asphodeline liburnica	🪴	☀ ☀		🪴	60	30	☐	Grey-green foliage
A. lutea	🪴	☀ ☀		🪴	120	30	▨	Dark green foliage. Fragrant flowers

 planting   *flowering*

Asphodelus
Asphodel
TUBEROUS ROOT

Similar to Asphodeline and from the same family, the asphodels produce long, dense spikes of delicate looking, starry flowers. They are found growing wild in open woodland and meadows in the Mediterranean.

The 2.5–4cm (1–1⅛in) wide flowers have prominent stamens and each of the six petals have a central vein – pink in *Asphodelus albus* and rust brown in *A. ramosus*. They look superb when grown among other plants in herbaceous or mixed borders, but asphodels are also extremely suitable for naturalizing in short grass, a wildflower garden or even

Asphodelus ramosus

growing in light shade planted among trees and shrubs.

The flower spikes emerge from dense clumps of

Asphodelus albus

soil	For best results, plant Asphodelus in any free draining, fertile soil
site	Grows well if positioned in either light or partial shade in the garden
planting	Plant these tuberous roots 10cm (4in) deep and roughly 30cm (12in) apart
general care	Cut back flowering stems after the flowers have faded and cut back the leaves in late autumn. Do not overfeed or overwater
pests & diseases	Relatively trouble free. Pests and diseases do not usually cause any problems to this plant

narrow, grass-like foliage which, in the case of *A. albus*, is a very attractive grey-green colour; the foliage of *A. ramosus* is mid green.

Plants can easily reach more than 1m (3ft) in height, with a spread of roughly half.

Although Asphodelus is generally not bothered by pests and diseases, keep an eye out for aphids, which can become fairly troublesome if left unchecked.

Native to the Mediterranean and Central Europe, these plants will need protection in winter where temperatures regularly fall below -5°C (23°F); Asphodelus plants overwintered outside should be given a generous layer of mulch, such as bark chippings or cocoa shells, in late autumn.

Asphodels are propagated by dividing the roots in early spring.

	SPRING	SUMMER	AUTUMN	WINTER	height (cm)	spread (cm)	flower colour	
Asphodelus albus		● ●			90	45	☐	Simple flower spikes
A. ramosus		● ●			120	45	☐	Branching flower stems

🌱 planting   ☀ flowering

Babiana
Baboon flower
CORM

The baboon flower is not a common sight in many gardens, except for in its native South Africa. The common name derives from the fact that baboons are said to eat the corms.

Babianas are valued for their clusters of brightly coloured 2.5cm (1in) wide flowers which resemble freesias, although the flower spikes are upright rather than arching.

Although the species have a limited colour range, races of *Babiana stricta* are available. These range from pearly white with a dark eye through to yellow, rose, red, mauve and indigo. Some named cultivars may also be offered by some specialist suppliers.

Although babianas can be grown outside in areas where the winter temperatures remain

soil	For best results, plant Babiana in any light, well-drained, humus-rich soil
site	Requires a warm, sheltered position, preferably in full sun
planting	Plant corms 15–20cm (6–8in) deep and space roughly 10cm (4in) apart
general care	Mulch plants that are overwintering outside or, better still, lift them in autumn and store indoors
pests & diseases	Relatively trouble free. Pests and diseases do not usually cause any problems to this plant

above -5°C (23°F), it is best to lift the corms in autumn or grow them as indoor pot plants.

If you intend to keep the corms outside all year, plant them 20cm (8in) deep to give them extra protection and mulch the soil with straw or leafmould. If you intend to lift them in the autumn, wait until the foliage dies down, then lift, clean and dry them, and store in dry sand or compost in frost-free conditions.

If growing babianas in pots, plant them 5cm (2in) deep in pots of loam-based compost. Keep the compost just moist when the plants are in growth and feed regularly up to flowering with a liquid fertilizer. Once the flowers have faded store the corms in a cool place in dry compost until planting time.

Plants can be propagated by carefully removing offsets, which are readily produced once the plants are dormant, and planting in mid-spring.

Babiana stricta 'Kew hybrids'

	SPRING	SUMMER	AUTUMN	WINTER	height (cm)	spread (cm)	flower colour	
Babiana plicata					20	10		Flowers are scented
B. stricta					30	10		Flowers are sometimes scented

 planting   flowering

Begonia
Tuberous begonia
TUBER

If you are searching for large, blousy blooms to brighten up the garden and containers for months on end during the summer until the first frosts, then look no further than the tuberous-rooted *Begonia* x *tuberhybrida* begonias.

Begonia 'Can-can'

Begonia 'Picotee'

There are two basic types of tuberous begonias: the bushy Multiflora Group, which are used for outdoor bedding, and the trailing Pendula Group that are perfect for growing in hanging baskets and window boxes. Some tuberhybrida cultivars produce enormous blooms – even up to the size of a dinner plate. To protect the blooms from becoming spoilt, these cultivars need protection from wind and rain, and are best grown in a greenhouse or similar protected environment. Plants and often the individual blooms will need staking. These are the exhibition cultivars seen at flower shows.

Flowers are available in a wide range of colours, and they may be single, semi-double or double, plain-edged or ruffled, single colours or bicolours.

Being natives of tropical forests, begonias thrive in shady positions, making them ideal for such areas of the garden where many other summer bedding plants would not grow well. Protection from strong winds is also a good idea, because both wind and sun can scorch the blooms and the foliage.

The tubers are bought in late winter or early spring and planted hollow side up. They are best started into growth from early spring onwards in a heated greenhouse or a month later in an unheated one. Press the tubers into trays of compost at a temperature of 15–18°C (60–65°F) and then transplant individually into small pots once the shoots have started to produce leaves. As the plants grow they may need potting into larger pots or they can be transplanted to hanging baskets.

Plants should be hardened off for 10 to 14 days before planting outside when the risk of frost has passed – usually in late spring or early summer. They can also be planted into their flowering positions in very late spring, but this results in a later start to flowering.

Begonias produce male and female flowers on the same plants. If you want big, showy blooms it pays to pinch out the small female flowers produced below the large male ones.

Begonia 'Roy Hartley'

soil	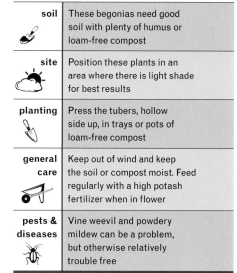	These begonias need good soil with plenty of humus or loam-free compost
site		Position these plants in an area where there is light shade for best results
planting		Press the tubers, hollow side up, in trays or pots of loam-free compost
general care		Keep out of wind and keep the soil or compost moist. Feed regularly with a high potash fertilizer when in flower
pests & diseases		Vine weevil and powdery mildew can be a problem, but otherwise relatively trouble free

To save tubers for replanting the following year, move plants in the autumn to a frost-free place when the foliage and stems start to die back. Allow them to die down completely and keep the soil or compost dry. Clean away any soil or compost and store the tubers in almost dry sand or soil-less compost in a cool, frost-free place.

Begonia tubers can be propagated by carefully cutting the tubers in half, ensuring each half has at least one bud or growth point. Dust the cuts with sulphur powder to prevent rots. However, it is much better to start the tubers into growth with heat and then take 7.5–10cm (3–4in) long shoots as cuttings (see pages 18–19).

Begonia 'Fairylight'

	SPRING	SUMMER	AUTUMN	WINTER	height (cm)	spread (cm)	flower colour	
Begonia 'Allan Langdon'					80	60		Exhibition
B. 'Can-can'					80	60		Exhibition. Picotee flowers with red rim
B. 'Fairylight'					80	60		Exhibition. Picotee flowers with red rim
B. 'Flamboyant'					30	30		Multiflora
B. 'Gold Doubloon'					80	60		Exhibition
B. Non-stop strain					30	30		Multiflora
B. 'Picotee'					30	30		Excellent for brightening up dark corners
B. Primadonna strain					35	30		Multiflora
B. 'Roy Hartley'					80	60		Exhibition
B. Sensation strain					30	60		Pendulous
B. 'Sugar Candy'					80	60		Exhibition
B. sutherlandii					30	60		Pendulous

 potting up   *planting*   ☀ *flowering*

Belamcanda

Leopard lily
RHIZOME

This member of the Iris family resembles the iris in habit – having sword-shaped leaves borne in fans on branching stems – and producing iris-like flowers. The spotted flowers give the plant its common name.

The attractive deep yellow or orange flowers have red or purple spots at their base and plants do well in flower borders or informal plantings. Plants reach 90cm (36in) in height, with a width of around 30cm (12in). Although each flower only lasts one day, a succession is produced over several weeks. *Belamcanda chinensis* will be in flower throughout the summer.

The resulting seed pods split open in autumn to reveal shining black seeds which give rise to the plant's other common name – blackberry lily. The seed pods are often used in dried flower arrangements.

Plant out in early to late spring. Although hardy to -15°C (5°F), plants will benefit from a thick winter mulch. Alternatively, you can grow them in pots indoors. Plant five rhizomes in a 15cm (6in) pot of loam-free compost to which extra sharp sand has been added. Keep the pots in the dark until growth starts, keep the compost just moist and feed fortnightly. When flowering has

soil	Belamcanda needs well-drained, humus-rich soil or loam-free compost
site	These plants grow well if positioned in a sunny position or in light shade
planting	Plant Belamcanda 2.5cm (1in) deep and around 12.5–15cm (5–6in) apart
general care	Mulch the soil in winter with compost, composted bark or leafmould to protect the rhizomes
pests & diseases	Relatively trouble free. Pests and diseases do not usually cause any problems to this plant

finished, stop watering and store the dry rhizomes for replanting the following spring.

Leopard lilies are easily propagated by dividing overcrowded clumps during spring.

Belamcanda chinensis

Brimeura

Spanish hyacinth
BULB

Looking very much like a more refined, diminutive bluebell – with which it used to be classified – the Spanish hyacinth is a charming bulb for planting in rockeries or for edging borders.

Being a native plant of mountain meadows, the Spanish hyacinth is perfect for rockeries and raised beds. It grows well in dappled shade, making it a perfect choice for shady rockeries, and even underplanting shrubs and herbaceous plants in beds and borders.

Because of its diminutive nature it is also an excellent plant for growing in small pots for colour in the greenhouse. In such situations the flowers can be appreciated even more.

soil	For best results, plant Brimeura in well-drained, humus-rich soil
site	Prefers to be in partial shade, but will also grow in a sunny position
planting	Plant the bulbs 10cm (4in) deep and space roughly 10cm (4in) apart
general care	Do not overfeed or overwater the plants when in growth, but otherwise relatively easy to grow and look after
pests & diseases	Relatively trouble free. Pests and diseases do not usually cause any problems to this plant

Brimeura amethystina 'Alba'

The fine, grassy foliage erupts in late spring and early summer to reveal the flower spikes, adorned with between 10 and 15 delicate-looking, 1cm (½in) long bluebell-like flowers.

The white-flowered form 'Alba' is even better for shady positions as this colour helps to lift and brighten up otherwise dark and dingy areas. It is also showier and, unusually, more vigorous than the blue-flowered species.

The bulbs are hardy down to -15°C (5°F), but where winter temperatures regularly dip down to -10°C (14°F), protect them with a thick mulch of bark or similar material.

Brimeuras are easily propagated by dividing established clumps when the foliage has died down and the bulbs are dormant in summer.

	SPRING	SUMMER	AUTUMN	WINTER	height (cm)	spread (cm)	flower colour	
Brimeura amethystina	flowering, flowering		planting, planting		25	10	[indigo]	Flowers may be indigo
B. amethystina 'Alba'	flowering, flowering		planting, planting		25	10	[white]	Showier and more vigorous

planting *flowering*

Bulbocodium
CORM

Bulbocodium vernum is a delightful species perfect for bringing a splash of colour to the garden in early spring or even winter. In the wild, bulbocodiums are found in alpine meadows and grassland in southern and eastern Europe.

Bulbocodium, sometimes referred to as the spring saffron, produces starry, funnel-shaped, virtually stemless flowers close to the ground. As a result it can be easily confused with colchicums (to which it is related) or crocuses.

Plant out in early to mid-autumn. The floral display normally gets going in early spring, but flowers can start appearing as early as mid-winter in mild regions, and continues for about three weeks. The dark green, arching leaves begin to emerge with the flowers, but only reach their full length after the blooms have finished. This is the habit that separates them from colchicums and crocuses. The foliage eventually reaches up to 15cm (6in) long and dies back in early to mid-summer.

Although native to alpine meadows in the Alps and Pyrenees in Europe, and perfectly hardy, the plants dislike excessive winter wet and so thrive in sunny rockeries, raised beds and well-drained beds and borders. Bulbocodium is also a perfect subject for growing in pots in a cold greenhouse or similar position.

Bulbocodium vernum

It can even be grown indoors where it will flower in mid- to late winter. Plant five or six corms in a bowl and keep them in a cool room until the flower buds start to appear. Then move the young plants to their flowering position.

Young offsets can be separated from the mature corms after the foliage has died down. It is a good idea to do this every two to three years to help maintain vigorous flowering.

Spring saffron makes a perfect partner if grown in clumps alongside the pure white of snowdrops (Galanthus), the golden yellow of winter aconite (*Eranthis hyemalis*), the blues of dwarf irises (*Iris reticulata*) and the whites of crocuses. Plant Bulbocodium at the base of box (Buxus) to brighten up this evergreen plant.

Bulbocodium vernum

Bulbocodium vernum

soil	For best results, plant Bulbocodium in any well-drained soil
site	Position these plants in a sunny position in the garden for good growth
planting	Plant Bulbocodium 7.5cm (3in) deep and space roughly 7.5cm (3in) apart
general care	Ensure the plants have good drainage and do not overwater because bulbocodiums do not like excessive wet
pests & diseases	Relatively trouble free. Pests and diseases do not usually cause any problems to this plant

Camassia
Quamash
BULB

An elegant plant with stately spikes clothed with star-shaped flowers, making camassias the perfect plants for beds and borders. The lovely star-shaped flowers of camassias are produced from late spring to early summer above tufts of long, narrow foliage.

Camassia's flower size varies from 4cm (1½in) wide up to 7.5cm (5in) on *Camassia leichtlinii*, and open first at the base of the flowering stems followed in succession by those higher up. *C. cusickii* can produce up to 100 blooms per spike.

soil	Will flourish if planted in humus-rich, moisture-retentive soil
site	Camassias grows best in a sunny position but they will tolerate light shade
planting	Plant these bulbs 10cm (4in) deep and space roughly 15cm (6in) apart
general care	Leave the bulbs undisturbed for several years for best results. Remove flower stems after flowering
pests & diseases	Relatively trouble free. Pests and diseases do not usually cause any problems to this plant

Camassia quamash

The foliage is usually bright green, although that of *C. cusickii* is grey-green, and dies down in late summer. It should be carefully removed when completely dead.

In the wild, camassias grow beside streams or in damp meadows. This means they need good, moisture-retentive soil in the garden and even grow well in heavy soils, but make sure it does not remain waterlogged in winter or the bulbs will rot. Water well in summer if the soil becomes dry.

Although they look great in beds and borders, camassias – especially *C. quamash* – will also grow well when naturalized in grass or even under trees.

Propagate by lifting mature clumps in late summer or early autumn and remove offsets, which should be replanted immediately.

	SPRING	SUMMER	AUTUMN	WINTER	height (cm)	spread (cm)	flower colour	
Camassia cusickii	● ●		✁ ✁		90	30		Grey-green foliage
C. leichtlinii	● ●		✁ ✁		90	30		Green foliage
C. leichtlinii subsp. *suksdorfii* Caerulea Group	● ●		✁ ✁		90	30		One of the best blue forms
C. quamash	● ●		✁ ✁		75	25		Best one for naturalizing

 planting   ● flowering

Canna
Indian shot
RHIZOME

One of the most popular plants for providing height in summer bedding schemes, cannas provide colour from their flowers, as well as their foliage. Indian shot is so called because the hard, black seeds were supposed to have been used for ammunition.

Canna indica 'Purpurea'

Canna 'Striata'

Canna 'President'

They are brazen plants, producing gloriously colourful displays from the brilliant trumpet-shaped flowers up to 15cm (6in) across on top of the erect stems, and their bold ornamental foliage up to 60cm (2ft) long, which is variously coloured. The flower colour ranges from pale yellow through pink to deep red and the foliage is either green, grey-green, purple or variegated which, in the case of *Canna* Tropicanna, is vivid purple, pink and orange.

As well as being perfect for beds and borders among herbaceous plants or for providing height in bedding schemes, cannas can also be grown in large containers for patios. Plant the rhizomes 2.5cm (1in) below the surface of the compost and keep well fed and watered throughout summer and early autumn. Bring the plants into a frost-free place after the first frost and repot the rhizomes into fresh compost in spring.

Despite their exotic look and half-hardy nature, cannas are fairly easy to grow, and just need watering during periods of extended drought. Feeding with a high potash liquid fertilizer during flowering will help extend the flowering period.

The rhizomes are bought from late winter to early spring. Although they can be planted directly outside in late spring it is far better to start them into growth in spring with heat. This produces good sized plants for planting outside in late spring or early summer – after the fear of frosts has passed – which establish quickly and come into flower earlier in the summer.

Pot-grown plants are available for planting directly outside during the summer.

Plants are not reliably winter hardy – although some gardeners in mild regions do keep them outside, first covering them with a thick mulch of bark or similar insulation – and are best lifted in late autumn and overwintered in a frost-free place. Not only is it risky to leave the plants outside during winter, if they do come through successfully they start into growth so late that the flowering display is either extremely late in the season or non-existent.

	soil	For best results, plant Canna in any good, humus-rich soil
	site	These plants need to be positioned in a warm, sunny site in the garden
	planting	Plant in pots of compost or directly into the garden 5cm (2in) deep and 30cm (12in) apart
	general care	Plant out after frosts, keep well fed to prolong flowering and water during prolonged drought. Lift plants after the first frosts
	pests & diseases	Relatively trouble free from pests and diseases. However, viruses are now becoming a problem

Canna 'Wyoming'

Canna Tropicanna

To overwinter plants indoors cut down the stems to ground level, then carefully lift the rhizomes, remove any soil or compost and trim away any dead growth. Then store in slightly moist compost or sand and keep the rhizomes in a frost-free place. Check the rhizomes periodically to ensure they do not shrivel and dry out or become too damp, which can encourage rotting. If this is the case, carefully cut off any rotten areas and dust the cuts with sulphur powder.

Propagate by dividing the rhizomes before potting up or plant directly outside in spring.

	SPRING	SUMMER	AUTUMN	WINTER	height (cm)	spread (cm)	flower colour
Canna 'Black Knight'	🪣🪣	🌱 ● ● ● ● ● ●			150	60	Purple-brown foliage
C. 'Cleopatra'	🪣🪣	🌱 ● ● ● ● ● ●			150	60	Foliage often splashed with black
C. 'Endeavour'	🪣🪣	🌱 ● ● ● ● ● ●			150	60	Foliage has glaucous sheen
C. indica 'Purpurea'	🪣🪣	🌱 ● ● ● ● ● ●			180	60	Purple foliage
C. 'King Humbert'	🪣🪣	🌱 ● ● ● ● ● ●			200	60	Bronze-red foliage
C. 'Lucifer'	🪣🪣	🌱 ● ● ● ● ● ●			45	25	Green foliage
C. 'Picasso'	🪣🪣	🌱 ● ● ● ● ● ●			100	50	Green foliage
C. 'President'	🪣🪣	🌱 ● ● ● ● ● ●			120	50	Blue-green foliage
C. 'Richard Wallace'	🪣🪣	🌱 ● ● ● ● ● ●			120	50	Bright green foliage
C. 'Striata'	🪣🪣	🌱 ● ● ● ● ● ●			90	50	Green and yellow striped foliage
C. 'Striped Beauty'	🪣🪣	🌱 ● ● ● ● ● ●			60	30	Bright green foliage veined creamy-white
C. Tropicanna = 'Phasion'	🪣🪣	🌱 ● ● ● ● ● ●			75	30	Vivid purple, pink and orange foliage
C. 'Wyoming'	🪣🪣	🌱 ● ● ● ● ● ●			120	50	Purple-brown foliage

 potting up   *planting*   ● *flowering*

Cardiocrinum

Giant lily

BULB

If you have the room and you want the jaws of your visitors to drop when they enter the garden, then *Cardiocrinum giganteum* (also known as *Lilium giganteum*) is just the plant for you!

The giant lily is an impressive and imposing plant that produces up to 20 lily-like trumpet flowers, 15cm (6in) long, in summer on stems up to 3.5m (11ft) tall that will tower above your head. The flowers are strongly fragrant and have reddish markings on the inside of the petals. The leaves are heart shaped and up to 45cm (18in) across.

Naturally this plant needs plenty of space in which to develop and grow. Being native of woodland in the Himalayas, China and Japan, Cardiocrinum is best grown in moist but well-drained, very fertile soil in partial shade. Like some true lilies, Cardiocrinum will not grow well in chalky soil.

Plant out in early autumn. You may need a little patience to enjoy this plant as the bulbs produce leafy rosettes that can take up to two years to become established and produce the flowering stems. In time they will flower in mid- to late summer. Plants will need watering during extended periods of hot, dry weather in summer. Add a general fertilizer in spring to improve flowering. Although pretty hardy it pays to protect new growth with a mulch of bark chippings in cold winters.

Unfortunately, giant lily bulbs die after flowering but produce bulblets before they do so. In autumn when the foliage has turned brown, dig up the plants, remove these bulblets and replant immediately. The bulblets will take three to five years to reach flowering size, so to ensure flowers every year plant bulbs over three successive years.

Cardiocrinum giganteum

soil	Cardiocrinum needs well-drained, but moisture-retentive, fertile soil
site	The giant lily grows best if planted in a position in partial shade
planting	Plant giant lily bulbs with the tip of the bulb level with the soil surface
general care	Once the foliage turns brown, lift the plants, remove the bulblets and replant them straight away
pests & diseases	Keep an eye out for aphids, botrytis and rot, as these can all be a problem to Cardiocrinum plants

Chionodoxa
Glory of the snow
BULB

Chionodoxas are delightful low growing bulbs that look especially glorious when growing through – and the blooms set off by – snow. However, flowering as they do in early spring, snow is not always guaranteed at this time.

These hardy plants are perfect for the rock garden, the front of the border, growing in front of, or as ground cover to, shrubs and other plants, as well as naturalizing in grass. The six-petalled, starry flowers are borne in loose sprays on upright stems and

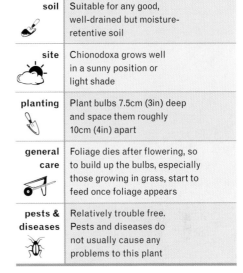

soil	Suitable for any good, well-drained but moisture-retentive soil
site	Chionodoxa grows well in a sunny position or light shade
planting	Plant bulbs 7.5cm (3in) deep and space them roughly 10cm (4in) apart
general care	Foliage dies after flowering, so to build up the bulbs, especially those growing in grass, start to feed once foliage appears
pests & diseases	Relatively trouble free. Pests and diseases do not usually cause any problems to this plant

emerge just before the broad, glossy, grass-like foliage appears.

The blooms last for up to four weeks and the foliage soon starts to die back once flowering has finished. The dainty flowers can be cut for indoor decoration, and plants can be grown in containers indoors when they will flower earlier in late winter.

Chionodoxa luciliae is the most commonly available type, producing one to three upward-facing flowers on each stem. Yet *C. forbesii* is often mis-named and sold under this name. This produces deep blue flowers in groups of between four and 12; it is also a much taller plant reaching up to 25cm (10in). 'Pink Giant' is a form of *C. forbesii*.

Plants are easily propagated by lifting the bulbs after the foliage has died down, separating the bulbs and replanting immediately. Plants also self-seed readily.

Chionodoxa sardensis

	SPRING	SUMMER	AUTUMN	WINTER	height (cm)	spread (cm)	flower colour	
Chionodoxa luciliae	● ●		✿ ✿		12.5	8		Flowers have a prominent white centre
C. 'Pink Giant'	● ●		✿ ✿		20	8		Flowers have a prominent white centre
C. sardensis	● ●		✿ ✿		15	8		Flowers have a small white eye

🌱 *planting* ✿ *flowering*

Chlidanthus
BULB

Chlidanthus fragrans deserves to be more widely grown for its delightfully scented flowers that appear in mid-summer, but it is not reliably hardy, which has often held back its popularity.

This species from South America produces slender flower stalks up to 25cm (10in) high topped with up to six lily-like blooms that are 7.5cm (3in) wide and sweetly scented. The attractive grey-green foliage appears shortly after the flowers.

When planting make sure you choose a position where the flowers can be readily appreciated and the scent enjoyed by passers by.

Bulbs can be planted outside permanently in gardens that remain frost free (or almost so) in winter and will usually need a mulch of bark for protection. However, in areas where frosts are expected you will have to adopt another approach to cultivation. You can lift the bulbs in mid- to late autumn and store the bulbs in a dry, cool but frost-free place ready for planting outside again in spring. Alternatively, pot up the bulbs in a loam-based compost and grow in a cool greenhouse or conservatory at 5–10°C (40–50°F). Another option is to grow Chlidanthus in pots that are then plunged in the garden after the fear of frosts in late spring for flowering in summer and then lifted again in the autumn.

soil	For best results, plant these in a good, well-drained soil or compost
site	Chlidanthus needs a sunny position, preferably at the base of a wall
planting	Plant with nose of the bulb just above soil level, 15cm (6in) apart in the garden, or three in a pot
general care	Lift the bulbs in late autumn and store somewhere cool and dry for planting out again in mid-spring
pests & diseases	Relatively trouble free. Pests and diseases do not usually cause any problems to this plant

Apart from winter care, these plants are easy to look after. They do need plenty of water when growing, but reduce watering after flowering and start to dry off the bulbs as the foliage dies down.

Plants are propagated by removing offsets in spring before planting; they will flower in three years.

Chlidanthus fragrans

Colchicum
Autumn crocus
or Meadow
saffron
CORM

If you are looking for plants to brighten up the dreary autumn days in the garden, then you cannot do much better than choosing colchicums, with their brightly coloured flowers.

Although commonly called the autumn crocus because the flowers resemble the true crocus, colchicums are actually more closely related to lilies. The flowers are produced at ground level, because they arise directly from the corm without a true stem. The larger flowered species will produce around one to three flowers per corm, whereas the small flowered forms like *Colchicum byzantinum*, can produce anything up to 20 blooms.

Colchicums are ideal for growing in rock gardens, planting near and under shrubs, as well as naturalizing in grass. In the latter case it is important to choose vigorous types, such as *C. autumnale*, but even these will not increase in size and number as well as those grown elsewhere. Smaller types, such as *C. agrippinum*, are best suited for warm, sunny borders.

The one drawback of colchicums is their large leaves that appear after the flowers and extend into spring, dying back in summer when the corms become dormant. However, by careful placement – growing them close to other plants that will hide

Colchicum 'Lilac Wonder'

soil	For best results, plant Colchicum in good, well-drained, humus-rich soil	
site	Colchicum grows well if positioned in either full sun or light shade	
planting	Plant the corms 10cm (4in) deep and space roughly 10–15cm (4–6in) apart	
general care	Flowers can be spoiled by the wind and rain, so plant closely together or give some support	
pests & diseases	Slugs and snails can be a problem, but otherwise these plants are relatively trouble free from pests and diseases	

Colchicum speciosum

Colchicum tenorei

the foliage in spring – you can easily get around this problem. When growing in grass it is important not to mow the foliage until it has died down, which can result in the grass turning yellow.

It is important to keep the foliage growing well until it starts to die back, which may mean extra watering during dry weather. If a feed is needed use a high potash one; high nitrogen fertilizers can produce even larger leaves.

Some of the large-flowered types can topple and become damaged by heavy rain, so plant close together to support each other. All parts of the plant are poisonous, too.

Plants are propagated by removing offsets when plants are dormant in summer and replanting immediately.

	SPRING	SUMMER	AUTUMN	WINTER	height (cm)	spread (cm)	flower colour	
Colchicum agrippinum					10	8		Small flowers with chequered markings
C. autumnale					15	15		Small flowers
C. autumnale 'Nancy Lindsay'					12.5	15		Flowers larger than the species
C. byzantinum					15	10		Flowers are open and funnel shaped
C. 'Lilac Wonder'					20	15		Flowers have a light checkering
C. 'Pink Goblet'					20	20		Large flowers
C. 'Rosy Dawn'					20	15		Large, fragrant flowers
C. speciosum					23	20		Robust species
C. speciosum 'Album'					20	30		Flowers are sturdy and weather resistant
C. tenorei					15	15		Grows best in dry shade under trees
C. 'Violet Queen'					25	25		Large flowers
C. 'Waterlily'					15	15		Large, fully double flowers

 planting flowering

Corydalis
TUBER

The attractive spikes of tubular, long-spurred flowers above lovely delicate, often ferny, foliage gives corydalis two good reasons to be planted in the garden. Looking like a small larkspur, but belonging to the poppy family, Corydalis are a beautiful choice for cool, partially shaded positions.

The spurred flowers are up to 3cm (1¼in) long and produced over several weeks in spring. The delicate foliage adds to the attraction but careful planting is needed to ensure other plants do not swamp them and where

Corydalis solida

Corydalis solida subsp. *incisa*

they are unlikely to be disturbed by regular soil cultivation. Try them in borders, rock gardens, under shrubs or in pots in a cool greenhouse.

The tubers usually double or treble in number each year, so good-sized clumps are soon produced. This makes them the perfect choice for ground cover especially under and around other plants that flower at the same time.

When growing in pots use a mixture of equal parts loam-based compost, peat or peat substitute and sharp sand. Plunge the pots up to their necks in damp sand or similar to insulate the roots from high temperatures. Repot annually in early spring.

Propagate by dividing overcrowded clumps before the foliage dies down in summer or after flowering in spring. Plants also readily self-seed and seedlings often appear in cracks in patios or old walls and brickwork.

soil	For best results, plant Corydalis in any moist, humus-rich soil
site	These plants will grow particularly well if positioned in partial shade
planting	Plant the tubers 7.5cm (3in) deep and space roughly 10cm (4in) apart
general care	The tubers should never be allowed to dry out in winter, but they do need partial drying out in summer
pests & diseases	Slugs and snails can be a problem, but otherwise these plants are relatively trouble free from pests and diseases

	SPRING	SUMMER	AUTUMN	WINTER	height (cm)	spread (cm)	flower colour	
Corydalis cava	● ● ●		🌱 🌱 🌱		20	15		Pale green foliage
C. solida	● ● ●		🌱 🌱 🌱		20	20		Flowers may be pink, red or purple. Grey-green foliage
C. solida subsp. *incisa*	● ● ●		🌱 🌱 🌱		20	20		Flowers may be pink or red. Olive-green foliage
C. solida subsp. *solida* 'George Baker'	● ● ●		🌱 🌱 🌱		20	20		Scented flowers. Grey-green foliage

🌱 planting   ● flowering

Crinum
BULB

The large trumpet-shaped flowers of crinums bring an exotic touch to gardens in late summer and early autumn. They produce large umbels of showy, funnel-shaped and often scented flowers.

This is a stately plant that is hardy down to around -5°C (23°F). To ensure they come through cold winters, however, it is essential they are planted in a warm position – preferably at the base of a warm wall or similar protected place.

The large 15cm (6in) bulbs produce strong stems at the top of which emerge the 15cm (6in) wide, 12.5cm (5in) long, sweetly smelling, lily-like flowers. The six petals have a satiny look to them. Each bulb will produce three to four stems each one bearing up to 10 flowers. Plant three or more bulbs closely together for a dramatic display.

soil	The plants need a well-drained, but moisture-retentive, humus-rich soil in which to thrive
site	A sheltered, warm and sunny position is the preferred choice for crinums
planting	Plant the bulbs 15cm (6in) deep and space roughly 45cm (18in) apart
general care	Water and feed regularly with a high potash fertilizer in summer. Remove flowers when they fade
pests & diseases	Relatively trouble free. Pests and diseases do not usually cause any problems to this plant

Crinum x powellii 'Album'

Once planted the bulbs should be left undisturbed for several years if possible as they may take a long time to settle in again.

Where winter temperatures are too low for the plants to grow outside, grow them in pots of a loam-based compost in a cool but frost-free greenhouse or conservatory. Plant with the tip of the bulb just above the surface of the compost. The pots can then be moved outside in early to mid-summer to flower, but brought inside again in autumn before the first frosts. Alternatively, the pots can be kept inside but ensure the glass is shaded from strong sunlight.

Outdoor plants should be protected in winter by covering with bark, straw or similar and covered with horticultural fleece to protect their exposed necks which sit above soil level.

Plants can be propagated by dividing the clumps in spring.

	SPRING	SUMMER	AUTUMN	WINTER	height (cm)	spread (cm)	flower colour	
Crinum x powellii	planting planting	flowering flowering			90	60	▦	Plant behind shrubs to hide the foliage
C. x powellii 'Album'	planting planting	flowering flowering			90	60	☐	Plant against a dark background to show off the flowers

planting   flowering

Crocosmia

Montbretia
CORM

Crocosmia is an old cottage garden favourite that has been grown for years and newer cultivars have now revived it as a trendy garden plant. The species *Crocosmia* x *crocosmiiflora* is sometimes listed under its old name of *Montbretia crocosmiiflora*.

C. x *crocosmiiflora* and *C. masoniorum* produce small flowers over a reasonably short time in summer. However, in recent years extensive breeding has resulted in a large number of cultivars with bigger flowers on longer spikes, in a wider range of colours and an extended flowering period. And this has ensured crocosmias' popularity in the garden, where they are best planted in herbaceous or mixed borders, but they also still look good in cottage gardens.

soil	Needs a well-drained, humus-rich soil that does not dry out in summer
site	Crocosmia prefers a sheltered, sunny or lightly shaded position
planting	Plant the corms 10cm (4in) deep and space out roughly 10–15cm (4–6in) apart
general care	Remove flowers once they fade. Divide overcrowded clumps every three to four years, but do not separate strings of corms
pests & diseases	Dry rot, leaf spot disease can be troublesome and red spider mite can be a problem in hot weather

Crocosmia 'Lucifer'

Crocosmia 'Spitfire'

Crocosmia 'Severn Sunrise'

The hooded, funnel-shaped flowers are borne on arching stems among sword-like foliage. Plants soon produce large clumps with many flowering stems so these plants can be guaranteed to bring a bright splash of colour to the garden. The species have orange or orange-red flowers, but cultivars range from yellow through orange to deep red often with a contrasting colouring.

Small-flowered cultivars produce a large number of slender blooms 3–4cm (1¼–1⅛in) across, those with large flowers bear a succession of broad-petalled blooms 6–8cm (2½–3¼in) across. Those with small flowers are more vigorous and increase quickly, whereas those with larger flowers are more showy but less vigorous, slightly less hardy and slower to increase.

Although fairly drought tolerant, they flower better if regularly watered in hot, dry periods. And although hardy – down to -5°C to -10°C (23–14°F) – they do not like long periods of extended frost, so will benefit from mulching in cold, exposed areas, especially the large-flowered cultivars.

Plant the corms in groups of at least five to seven, and plant on a layer of sharp sand or grit in heavy clay soils to improve winter drainage and prevent the corms rotting. Pot-grown plants are widely available and

Crocosmia x crocosmiiflora 'Solfatare'

can be planted in either autumn or spring. In fact, spring is best in colder regions.

The flower stems can be cut as the buds are opening for indoor display and last a long time in water.

Propagate by dividing clumps in spring before growth starts. This can be carried out every two to three years for cultivars and every four to five years for species.

	SPRING	SUMMER	AUTUMN	WINTER	height (cm)	spread (cm)	flower colour	
Crocosmia x *crocosmiiflora* 'Canary Bird'	✿ ✿	●	●		75	15		Small flowers
C. x *crocosmiiflora* 'Carmin Brillant'	✿ ✿	●	●		60	10		Small flowers on dark stems
C. x *crocosmiiflora* 'Citronella'	✿ ✿	●	●		60	10		Small flowers
C. x *crocosmiiflora* 'Emily Mckenzie'	✿ ✿	●	●		60	10		Large flowers with red marks
C. x *crocosmiiflora* 'Jackanapes'	✿ ✿	●	●		60	20		Small flowers
C. x *crocosmiiflora* 'Solfatare'	✿ ✿	●	●		60	10		Bronze-green foliage
C. x *crocosmiiflora* 'Star of the East'	✿ ✿	●	●		90	15		Large flowers
C. 'Emberglow'	✿ ✿	●	●		90	15		Small flowers on deep red stems
C. 'Honey Angels'	✿ ✿	● ● ●			60	10		Large flowers
C. 'Lucifer'	✿ ✿	●	●		120	25		Large flowers
C. 'Mars'	✿ ✿	● ● ●	●		75	10		Large flowers
C. masoniorum	✿ ✿	●	●		120	40		Small flowers
C. masoniorum 'Rowallane Yellow'	✿ ✿	● ● ●			80	15		Large flowers
C. 'Severn Sunrise'	✿ ✿	●	●		75	10		Small flowers
C. 'Spitfire'	✿ ✿	●	●		80	10		Small flowers

 planting   ● flowering

Crocus
CORM

Crocuses bring a welcome splash of colour to gardens – usually in spring – heralding the end of winter and the start of warmer weather. Although regarded as spring-flowering plants, some species of crocus flower in the autumn and others in winter.

By planting a range of Crocus species, you could have flowers for almost nine months. All produce funnel-shaped, six-petalled flowers on short stems low down to the ground. The flowers, which open and close with sunlight, are available in a wide range of colours, often with a colour contrast between the inner and outer petals and often with contrasting markings. In some species the flowers open out wide, but others remain goblet shaped. Many species produce scented flowers.

The narrow, grass-like foliage usually has a central white or grey stripe and grows longer as the flowers fade. Some of the autumn-flowering species produce leaves after the flowers, but in the spring-flowering types they appear together.

soil	Crocuses grow the best when planted in any well-drained soil
site	These plants can be grown in a position in either the sun or light shade
planting	Plant corms 7.5–10cm (3–4in) deep and space out 7.5–10cm (3–4in) apart
general care	Try to keep corms dry during their summer dormancy. Apart from that, these plants require little general care
pests & diseases	Usually disease free, however, squirrels and mice eat the corms, and birds may damage the flowers

Crocus chrysanthus 'Blue Pearl'

Crocus tommasinianus 'Whitewell Purple'

Crocus sieberi 'Bowles' White'

C. chrysanthus 'Cream Beauty'

All crocuses are suitable for growing as edging for beds and borders, in a rock garden, under trees, in containers and some of the more vigorous types, such as *Crocus speciosus*, *C. tommasinianus* and *C. vernus*, can be naturalized in grassland. They look best when planted in large groups or drifts of one type. Growing in pots allows you to appreciate the flowers close up and also gives the opportunity of keeping the compost dry during their summer dormancy.

And if you want to enjoy the flowers inside the house, cultivars of *C. chrysanthus* and *C. vernus* can be forced.

The first of the winter-flowering species is *C. laevigatus*, which starts blooming in early winter. This is followed by *C. imperati*, which has a long flowering period – mid- to late winter. *C. angustifolius* starts to flower in late winter.

Of the spring crocuses, *C. chrysanthus* starts to flower in late winter, continuing its

	SPRING	SUMMER	AUTUMN	WINTER	height (cm)	spread (cm)	flower colour	
Crocus angustifolius	flowering		planting	flowering	8	4		Outer petals have purple-brown mark
C. banaticus		planting	flowering		10	5		Inner petals smaller and paler
C. chrysanthus	flowering		planting	flowering	10	5		Flowers striped with maroon
C. chrysanthus 'Blue Pearl'	flowering		planting	flowering	10	5		Inner petals have pale brown base
C. chrysanthus 'Cream Beauty'	flowering		planting	flowering	10	5		Flowers rounded
C. chrysanthus 'E A Bowles'	flowering		planting	flowering	10	5		Throat is dark bronze
C. chrysanthus 'Ladykiller'	flowering		planting	flowering	10	5		Outer petals have deep purple mark
C. chrysanthus 'Snow Bunting'	flowering		planting	flowering	10	5		Outer petals have deep brown mark
C. chrysanthus 'Zwanenburg Bronze'	flowering		planting	flowering	10	5		Outer petals have purple-bronze mark
C. corsicus	flowering		planting		10	4		Outer petals are buff with purple stripe
C. goulimyi		planting	flowering		12	5		Funnel-shaped flowers
C. goulimyi subsp. *goulimyi* 'Mani White'		planting	flowering		12	5		Funnel-shaped flowers
C. imperati			planting	flowering	8	4		Outer petals are biscuit coloured marked with violet

planting flowering

Crocus sieberi subsp. *sublimis* 'Tricolor'

Crocus vernus 'Jeanne d'Arc'

display into spring, and is smaller and more graceful than *C. vernus*, flowering slightly later and into mid-spring. *C. x luteus* and *C. sieberi* are also included with the late winter flowering types. *C. corsicus* and *C. tommasinianus* start flowering in early spring.

The first of the autumn flowerers is *C. banaticus*, which starts in early autumn. This is followed by *C. goulimyi* and *C. kotschyanus* in mid-autumn and *C. ochroleucus* in late autumn. *C. speciosus* has the longest flowering period and may flower throughout autumn.

The most commonly planted crocuses are the cultivars of *C. chrysanthus*, which are often hybrids of it with *C. biflorus*, and the much-loved Dutch crocuses – cultivars of *C. vernus*. The latter are taller and larger than *C. chrysanthus* reaching 20cm (8in) high and having flowers up to 8cm (3¼in) long.

Plants are propagated by removing offsets when the leaves die back.

	SPRING	SUMMER	AUTUMN	WINTER	height (cm)	spread (cm)	flower colour	
C. kotschyanus		planting	flowering		8	4		Flowers have purple veins
C. laevigatus			planting	flowering	8	4		Flowers tinted yellow or purple
C. x luteus 'Golden Yellow'	flowering		planting	flowering	12	5		Large flowers
C. ochroleucus		planting	flowering		8	3		Flowers have yellow throat
C. sieberi	flowering		planting	flowering	10	3		Flowers have deep yellow throat
C. sieberi 'Albus'	flowering		planting	flowering	10	3		Flowers have orange throat
C. speciosus		planting	flowering		15	5		Flowers have white or yellow throat
C. speciosus 'Albus'		planting	flowering		15	5		Pure white flowers
C. tommasinianus	flowering		planting		10	3		Flowers may be white or purple
C. tommasinianus 'Whitewell Purple'	flowering		planting		10	3		Flowers silver-mauve within
C. vernus 'Jeanne d'Arc'	flowering		planting	flowering	15	5		Flowers have deep purple base
C. vernus 'Pickwick'	flowering		planting	flowering	15	5		Flowers have violet stripes and base
C. vernus 'Purpureus Grandiflorus'	flowering		planting	flowering	15	5		Larger flowers
C. 'Zephyr'		planting	flowering		20	5		Very large flowers

🌱 planting   ✺ flowering

Cyclamen

Hardy cyclamen
TUBER

The hardy cyclamen make delightful groundcover plants under trees and shrubs and, by choosing species carefully, you can have flowers lasting from late summer through to late spring.

Cyclamen coum 'Silver Leaf'

These hardy cyclamen are not to be confused with their larger flowered relatives grown as houseplants. The elegant flowers in shades of pink, crimson, mauve and white have gracefully reflexed petals and are held above the heart-shaped or rounded leaves. The latter often have fine white or silver marbling which adds to the overall attraction. Because the foliage lasts for some time it helps sustain a long period of interest.

Cyclamen are perfect for naturalizing among trees and shrubs, or for growing on rock gardens and in containers.

Although you can buy dried tubers in the autumn, they are sometimes reluctant to

soil	This plant requires a well-drained but moist, humus-rich soil
site	For Cyclamen to perform at its best, find a position in partial shade
planting	Plant 2.5–5cm (1–2in) deep, apart from *C. repandum*, which should be planted 7.5cm (3in) deep
general care	Top dress the soil annually with leafmould or compost and add a little bonemeal to add to the nutrients
pests & diseases	Vine weevil, eelworm and aphids may be a problem, but otherwise fairly free from pests and diseases

produce abundant growth if they have been dried for too long. It is far better to buy potted plants in growth. Whichever form of planting material you choose ensure the tubers are from cultivated stocks and not taken from the wild since wild collection has almost led to the extinction of some species. Once planted try not to disturb the plants for several years as they can be slow to establish.

Unlike other plants the tubers of cyclamen cannot be cut into sections so the only way to increase your stock is to buy new tubers. Most species do self-seed quite reliably and dense stands of plants can be built up in this way.

Cyclamen coum 'Album'

	SPRING	SUMMER	AUTUMN	WINTER	height (cm)	spread (cm)	flower colour	
Cyclamen cilicium		🌱 🌱	● ● ●		7.5	10		Deep green foliage marked with grey or creamy white
C. coum	●	🌱 🌱 🌱		● ● ●	10	20		Different leaf colours available
C. coum Pewter Group	●	🌱 🌱 🌱		● ● ●	10	20		Foliage is pewter often with a green margin
C. hederifolium		🌱 🌱 ● 🌱 ● ● ● ●			15	20		Foliage is grey-green with grey, cream or silver
C. purpurascens		🌱 ● 🌱 ● 🌱 ●			10	15		Green foliage with faint silvery-green markings
C. repandum	● ● ●	🌱 🌱 🌱			12.5	15		Toothed dark green foliage with silvery-grey markings

🌱 *planting*   ● *flowering*

Cyrtanthus

Scarborough lily
BULB

The Scarborough lily makes an elegant pot plant for indoor flowering where its large, slightly fragrant flowers will help brighten up a light windowsill or conservatory. Although there are several species of Cyrtanthus, the Scarborough lily (*Cyrtanthus elatus*) is the only one that is usually offered and grown.

It has a tortuous history of names, including being classified as *Vallota speciosa, C. purpureus* and *C. speciosus*. Although hardy down to -5°C (23°F), it is rarely grown outside where it would need to be sited at the base of a warm, sunny wall, but is usually restricted for indoor culture where it is much easier to look after. Although another option would be to grow it in a pot

soil	Plant in a loam-based compost with added humus and sharp sand
site	Needs a position in good light that receives some direct sunlight
planting	Plant with the tip of the bulb just above compost level, one bulb per 12.5–15cm (5–6in) pot
general care	Keep the compost moist and feed weekly with a liquid fertilizer when the plants are in growth
pests & diseases	Mealy bug can be a problem indoors, otherwise pests and diseases do not usually cause any problems to this plant

Cyrtanthus elatus

and move the pot into the garden during flowering bringing it back under cover before the first frosts in autumn.

The scarlet, 10cm (4in) wide trumpet-like flowers are produced in clusters up to nine in number at the top of thick stems. These are surrounded by the green, strap-shaped, evergreen basal leaves, which can be up to 45cm (18in) long.

After flowering, water sparingly, especially in winter. Keep the compost dry but not arid. Plants will need a minimum temperature of 4–8°C (39–46°F). Top dress the container with fresh compost when growth resumes. Plants flower best when potbound, so do not repot until absolutely necessary and then into a pot that is not too big.

Plants can be propagated by carefully removing offsets in spring.

	SPRING	SUMMER	AUTUMN	WINTER	height (cm)	spread (cm)	flower colour	
Cyrtanthus elatus		● ● ●			50	30		Flowers are slightly fragrant
C. 'Pink Diamond'		● ● ●	● ●		45	30		Flowers are unscented

planting   ● flowering

Dahlia
TUBEROUS ROOT

Dahlias come in such a wide range of heights, colours and flower types, and flower for so long in summer and autumn, that there is little that can beat them for bringing colour, form and interest to gardens.

Dahlia 'Allan Sparkes'

Apart from garden decoration, dahlias are excellent for cutting for flower arrangements and make a dramatic sight at autumn flower shows where they are exhibited in fiercely fought competitions. Most types can also be grown in large containers, although those growing no taller than

soil	Dahlias will perform at their best in any fertile, well-drained soil
site	Requires a position that receives several hours of direct sunshine
planting	Plant 7.5–10cm (3–4in) deep. Put tall cultivars 90cm (3ft) apart and short ones 30cm (1ft) apart
general care	Water thoroughly during dry spells, especially once the flower buds form, and mulch to maintain soil moisture
pests & diseases	Slugs, snails, aphids, earwigs, capsid bugs and viruses can be a problem. Grey mould and rots can affect tubers in store

Dahlia 'Gallery Art Deco'

90cm (3ft) high look much better for display on the patio.

Dahlia blooms are more complex than you may first imagine. They are made up of miniature flowers known as florets, with the type of floret present being a key to identification. The outer florets are called rays, the next layer are called collars and the inner ones are either tubular or disc; not all will be present in all types.

The range of cultivars and flower shape and size is so enormous – ranging from the giant decoratives down to the dwarf bedding and lilliput dahlias. To help with classification, dahlias are divided into several groups depending on their flower shape and make-up, and then

Dahlia 'Gallery Art Nouveau'

Dahlia 'Honka'

Dahlia 'Lilac Taratahi'

Dahlia merckii

further dub-divided according to flower size. The Royal Horticultural Society and National Dahlia Society divide them into the following categories.

Group 1 Singles. One ring of ray florets, central group of disc florets.
Group 2 Anemone-flowered. One or more rings of ray florets, central group of tubular florets.
Group 3 Collerette. One outer ring of flat ray florets, an inner ring of collar florets and a central group of disc florets.
Group 4 Waterlily. Fully double, flattened flowers. The ray florets may be flat or with slightly curved margins.
Group 5 Decorative. Fully double. The flat ray florets are broad with a blunt end.
Group 6 Ball. Fully double, ball-shaped flowers. The ray florets are rolled inwards on themselves. Group 6A is the small balls (flowers 10–15cm/4–6in in diameter) and 6B consists of the miniature balls (up to 10cm/4in).
Group 7 Pompon. Fully double, globe-shaped flowers. The ray florets are rolled inwards on themselves
Group 8 Cactus. Fully double. The ray florets are rolled outwards on themselves, narrow and pointed.
Group 9 Semi-cactus. Fully double. The pointed ray florets are rolled outwards on themselves for half their length or less.

Dahlia 'Pearl of Heemstede'

Group 10 Miscellaneous. This group includes all other dahlias not classified above such as the orchid-flowering, botanical, dwarf bedding, fimbriated and lilliput.

Cultivars in groups 4, 5, 8 and 9 are further divided by flower size, with A being giant (25.4cm/10in or larger), B large (20.3–25.4cm/ 8–10in), C medium (15.2–20.3cm/6–8in), D small (10.2–15.2cm/4–6in) and E miniature (up to 10.2cm/4in diameter), although there are no giants in group 4.

Dahlia 'Moonfire'

	SPRING	SUMMER	AUTUMN	WINTER	height (cm)	spread (cm)	flower colour	
Dahlia 'Allan Sparkes'	🌱 🪴🪴 🪴 ● ● ●	● ● ●			140	50		Group 4D
D. 'Alva's Doris'	🌱 🪴🪴 🪴 ● ● ●	● ● ●			120	60		Group 9D
D. 'Alva's Supreme'	🌱 🪴🪴 🪴 ● ● ●	● ● ●			140	60		Group 5A
D. 'Asahi Chohje'	🌱 🪴🪴 🪴 ● ● ●	● ● ●			100	50		Group 2
D. 'Aylett's Gaiety'	🌱 🪴🪴 🪴 ● ● ●	● ● ●			60	35		Group 5E
D. 'Bishop of Llandaff'	🌱 🪴🪴 🪴 ● ● ●	● ● ●			110	45		Group 10
D. 'Brookfield Delight'	🌱 🪴🪴 🪴 ● ● ●	● ● ●			70	45		Group 10. Single lilliput
D. 'Candy Cupid'	🌱 🪴🪴 🪴 ● ● ●	● ● ●			110	60		Group 6B
D. 'Clair de Lune'	🌱 🪴🪴 🪴 ● ● ●	● ● ●			100	60		Group 3
D. 'Dark Stranger'	🌱 🪴🪴 🪴 ● ● ●	● ● ●			140	75		Group 8C
D. 'Ellen Huston'	🌱 🪴🪴 🪴 ● ● ●	● ● ●			60	40		Group 10. Dwarf bedding
D. 'Fascination'	🌱 🪴🪴 🪴 ● ● ●	● ● ●			90	40		Group 10. Small waterlily dwarf bedding
D. 'Figurine'	🌱 🪴🪴 🪴 ● ● ●	● ● ●			150	60		Group 4D
D. 'Gallery Art Deco'	🌱 🪴🪴 🪴 ● ● ●	● ● ●			70	40		Group 5D
D. 'Gallery Art Nouveau'	🌱 🪴🪴 🪴 ● ● ●	● ● ●			70	40		Group 5E

 potting up 🌱 *planting* ● *flowering*

spring or potted up and grown on in a frost-free greenhouse, conservatory or similar and planted out when the danger of frosts has passed. However, they are best started into growth in trays of compost with heat and the resulting shoots used as cuttings that are grown on and planted out after frosts have gone (see pages 18–19). Plants treated in this way will be more vigorous and will start to flower earlier in the summer. How late in the autumn they continue to flower will depend on when cold weather or frosts begin.

All but the shortest of cultivars will benefit from staking, which is essential for tall plants producing large blooms. Always put the stake in place before planting to prevent damaging the tubers. To make bushier plants with more flowers, pinch out all the growing points about three weeks after planting. For larger flowers – especially if you intend showing them – remove the side buds in each flower cluster to leave just the terminal bud. Regular watering and feeding is needed to ensure a succession of blooms. Deadheading as the flowers fade will encourage further flushes of flowers.

When the first frosts have blackened the foliage it is time to lift the tubers for overwintering indoors. In mild areas you can risk leaving them in the ground, but there is

Dahlia 'So Dainty'

Dahlia 'Wandy'

All dahlias – even the dwarf bedding types – produce tubers. These can be bought from late winter to early spring, although the dwarf bedding cultivars are normally grown from seed. The tubers can be planted directly in the ground from mid- to late

	SPRING	SUMMER	AUTUMN	WINTER	height (cm)	spread (cm)	flower colour
D. 'Garden Party'	planting, potting up	flowering	flowering		70	40	Group 10. Medium cactus dwarf bedding
D. 'Geerlings Indian Summer'	planting, potting up	flowering	flowering		120	60	Group 9C
D. 'Glorie van Heemstede'	planting, potting up	flowering	flowering		125	60	Group 4D
D. 'Hamari Accord'	planting, potting up	flowering	flowering		120	60	Group 9B
D. 'Hamari Gold'	planting, potting up	flowering	flowering		120	60	Group 5A
D. 'Hamari Rose'	planting, potting up	flowering	flowering		120	60	Group 6B
D. 'Hamari Sunshine'	planting, potting up	flowering	flowering		150	60	Group 5B
D. 'Hillcrest Desire'	planting, potting up	flowering	flowering		125	60	Group 8D
D. 'Hillcrest Royal'	planting, potting up	flowering	flowering		110	60	Group 8C
D. 'Honka'	planting, potting up	flowering	flowering		100	60	Group 10
D. 'John Street'	planting, potting up	flowering	flowering		100	45	Group 4D
D. 'Kenora Valentine'	planting, potting up	flowering	flowering		160	60	Group 5B
D. 'Kidd's Climax'	planting, potting up	flowering	flowering		110	60	Group 5A
D. 'Lilac Taratahi'	planting, potting up	flowering	flowering		160	60	Group 8D
D. 'Lismore Willie'	planting, potting up	flowering	flowering		145	60	Group 4D

 potting up   planting   flowering

a chance they will be killed by heavy frosts or cold weather and plants will come into flower much later in the summer.

Use a fork to lift the plants from the soil, taking care not to damage the tubers. Tie a label with the cultivar name securely around each one. Cut off the old flowering stems to within 2.5cm (1in) from the base and trim away any thin roots. Remove the soil from the tubers by hand or wash it off. Then the remaining pieces of stem should be carefully split open with a knife. Alternatively, drill a hole through the base of the stem, to allow water to drain away. It is also a good idea to hang them upside down in a cool place for a week or so to dry off.

When dry, lightly dust the tubers with sulphur powder and place in trays or wooden boxes filled with dry sand, soil or compost, leaving only the old flower stems exposed. Place the trays in a cool but frost-free place. Inspect the tubers regularly and cut out any rot that develops with a clean, sharp knife and dust the cut surfaces with sulphur powder. If the tubers start to shrivel they should be plumped up by placing in a bucket of water, drying and then replacing in the storage medium.

Propagate plants by dividing the tubers at planting or from cuttings taken in spring.

Dahlia 'Wittemans Superba'

Dahlia 'Yellow Hammer'

	SPRING	SUMMER	AUTUMN	WINTER	height (cm)	spread (cm)	flower colour	
D. merckii					180	90		Group 10. Botanical
D. 'Minley Carol'					100	60		Group 7
D. 'Moonfire'					100	50		Group 10. Dwarf bedding
D. 'Nicola Jane'					100	45		Group 7
D. 'Pearl of Heemstede'					100	45		Group 5D
D. 'Small World'					110	60		Group 7
D. 'So Dainty'					100	60		Group 9E
D. 'Tally Ho'					75	45		Group 10
D. 'Wandy'					45	40		Group 7
D. 'Weston Pirate'					125	60		Group 8E
D. 'Weston Spanish Dancer'					125	60		Group 8E
D. 'Wittemans Superba'					125	60		Group 9D
D. 'Wootton Cupid'					110	60		Group 6B
D. 'Wootton Impact'					120	60		Group 9C
D. 'Yellow Hammer'					60	45		Group 10. Single dwarf bedding

 potting up   *planting*   *flowering*

Dierama
Angel's fishing rod *or* Wand flower
CORM

With their arching stems of pendent flowers, dieramas are one of the most graceful of all the members of the iris family. The long slender leaves and wiry stems of this elegant plant bowed down by 2.5cm (1in) long bell-shaped flowers look their best when arching over a pond or beside a path or similar garden position.

Planting close to a pond not only produces delightful reflections of the arching flower stems, but should also help provide added moisture which is necessary for healthy growth. The thin stems wave in the breeze, giving rise to the wand flower analogy.

The plants are easy to look after and once established require little in the way of care and attention. During extended hot and dry summer periods the soil may need to be kept moist.

Dieramas are often falsely accused of not being hardy, but they will tolerate temperatures as low as -10°C (23°F), providing the soil does not get waterlogged in winter. Even at such low temperatures the foliage stays evergreen, although it may die down when conditions are not to its liking.

soil	Dierama requires well-drained but moist, humus-rich soil
site	These plants need as warm a spot as possible, preferably in the full sun
planting	Plant the corms 7.5cm (3in) deep and space them roughly 30cm (12in) apart
general care	Remove faded flower stems and any dying foliage, otherwise these plants are fairly easy to care for
pests & disease	Thrips can be a problem, but otherwise these plants are relatively trouble free from pests and diseases

Dierama dracomontanum

Dierama dracomontanum is the baby of the family and is often sold under the name of *D. pumilum*.

Plants can be propagated by dividing clumps and replanting the corms in spring. But this plant dislikes disturbance, so only divide the clumps when it becomes absolutely necessary and there is a noticeable decline in flower quantity and quality. It may be better to carefully remove small, outer portions of the clump without lifting the whole plant.

	SPRING	SUMMER	AUTUMN	WINTER	height (cm)	spread (cm)	flower colour	
Dierama dracomontanum	🌱	● ●	🌱 🌱		75	30	▨	Flowers 2.5cm long
D. pendulum	🌱	●	🌱 🌱		120	30	▨	Flowers 2.5cm long
D pulcherrimum	🌱	● ●	🌱 🌱		150	45	▰	Flowers 5cm long

🌱 *planting*   ● *flowering*

Dracunculus

Dragon arum
TUBER

Not to everyone's liking, the distinctive dragon arum produces exotic looking flowers and leaves, but because of its rather pungent smell, it is a good idea to plant it away from the house or patio!

Dracunculus vulgaris is an intriguing plant and one that produces plenty of comment and interest when seen for the first time. The large flowers, which appear from early to mid-summer, consist of a large spathe and spadix (see page 33), the spathe being deep velvety purple and reaching up to 45cm (18in) in length, and the spadix is almost black. The dragon arum is sometimes listed as *Arum dracunculus*.

For the first few days the flower smells of rotting meat – used to attract pollinating insects – but this soon disappears. However, if the smell is likely to be a problem, simply plant it at the bottom of the garden or at least a few strides away from the house.

Everything about this plant is large. The leaves measure 20cm (8in) long and 35cm (14in) wide, making Dracunculus a perfect choice for a specimen plant in beds and borders, reaching 1.2m (4ft) tall. It can also be grown in large containers. The foliage is hand-shaped, and both it and the stems are dark green with white spots or stripes.

Plant out any time from early to late spring. Dracunculus is not completely hardy, so will need some protection in exposed gardens. You can either cover it with a mulch or a cloche or plant it at the base of evergreen shrubs, which should provided adequate cover.

Plants are propagated by removing offsets in late summer.

soil	For best results, plant Dracunculus in a good, well-drained soil
site	This plant prefers any position in full sun for it to really flourish
planting	Plant tubers 15cm (6in) deep and space them roughly 45cm (18in) apart
general care	Tubers may need winter protection in cold or exposed areas, but fairly easy to grow
pests & disease	Relatively trouble free. Pests and diseases do not usually cause any problems to this plant

Dracunculus vulgaris

Bulbs

Eranthis
Winter aconite
TUBER

Flowering at the same time as snowdrops, the winter aconite is a perfect companion to these plants and help brighten up dull winter days – especially when planted in bold groups.

Winter aconites produce brightly coloured, cup-shaped flowers above finely cut, bright green leaves and surrounded by a ruff of leaf-like bracts.

Eranthis is a woodland plant, which generally prefers cool conditions and can be grown in partially shaded beds and borders. It also makes superb ground cover under deciduous trees and shrubs, or alongside early-flowering perennials such as hellebores. It is best to plant near established plants, since the tubers need a dry summer dormancy.

Winter aconites can also be grown in light grass, in pots in a cold greenhouse or

soil	Eranthis will grow their best planted in any well-drained soil
site	Prefers a situation in either a sunny or partially shaded area of the garden
planting	Plant the tubers 5cm (2in) deep and space them roughly 10cm (4in) apart
general care	Soak tubers in tepid water for a few hours before planting or place in trays of damp compost for a week or so
pests & disease	Aphids can be a problem for these plants and birds will sometimes peck at the flowers

indoors for flowering in mid-winter onwards.

Eranthis hyemalis Cilicica Group and *E. hyemalis* Tubergenii Group 'Guinea Gold' tolerate more sun than the species and are suitable for humus-rich soil on rock gardens and even the front of sunny borders.

When planting add extra humus to the soil and then leave the plants to establish and colonize the area.

Plants do not always successfully establish from dried tubers, but you can buy pot-grown plants and some nurseries offer transplants lifted while still in leaf. This is known as 'in the green'. When buying dried tubers get them as early as possible in the autumn and plant immediately,

Plants are propagated by lifting the tubers immediately after flowering and still in full leaf. The plants of *E. hyemalis* will also readily self-seed, sometimes to the point of being a nuisance.

Eranthis hyemalis

	SPRING	SUMMER	AUTUMN	WINTER	height (cm)	spread (cm)	flower colour	
Eranthis hyemalis	●		✿ ✿	● ●	10	10		Flowers up to 2.5cm across
E. hyemalis Cilicica Group	● ●		✿ ✿		10	10		New foliage is tinged bronze
E. hyemalis Tubergenii Group 'Guinea Gold'	●		✿ ✿	● ●	15	10		Large flowers

 planting ● flowering

Eremurus

Foxtail lily
TUBEROUS ROOT

In recent years the foxtail lilies have become much more popular as gardeners begin to realise just how impressive their huge flower spikes are. The stately tall spires of flowers create a magnificent garden display.

The garden trend for more exotic plants and flowers has certainly improved the popularity of Eremurus – which can only be a good thing. The heights listed in the table are the maximum, but plants may grow quite a bit shorter than this.

The flower spikes are made up of hundreds of small, starry flowers tightly packed together that put on an amazing display when fully open.

In the wild they grow in rocky, semi-desert, which gives a clue to the garden conditions needed. They do not like heavy soils that remain wet or waterlogged in winter and should either be grown in free-draining soils, in raised beds or on a bed of sharp sand with more sharp sand mixed into the covering soil.

Sadly, foxtail lilies are not completely hardy and so plants must be grown in a warm, sunny position and mulched in winter with sharp sand, ashes or similar during periods of prolonged cold. In areas that are very wet in winter, covering the plants with a cloche would give better results. But strangely enough they require some low temperatures in winter to flower well, and so should not be grown in areas that are completely frost free.

Eremurus cultivar

A number of hybrids and named cultivars reaching heights up to 2m (6½ft) are also available from specialist growers. They come in a range of colours from white through yellow and orange to pink and red shades. Look out for the Shelford hybrids, Highdown hybrids, as well as Ruiter's hybrids.

Plants can be propagated by carefully dividing the roots and replanting the crowns as the foliage dies back in late summer.

soil	These plants will thrive in any well-drained, humus-rich light soil
site	Eremurus needs a position that receives several hours of direct sunlight
planting	Plant the tuberous roots 7.5cm (3in) deep and space 60–90cm (2–3ft) apart
general care	Mulch the emerging foliage in spring to protect plants against late frosts. Stake tall plants
pests & disease	Slugs and snails may damage young growth, but apart from this, relatively trouble free

	SPRING	SUMMER	AUTUMN	WINTER	height (cm)	spread (cm)	flower colour	
Eremurus robustus		● ●	✎ ✎		300	100		Flowers marked with brown and green
E. stenophyllus		● ●	✎ ✎		150	75		Flowers fade to orangey brown
E. stenophyllus subsp. *stenophyllus*		● ●	✎ ✎		120	60		Leaves and stems are smooth
E. 'Yellow Giant'		● ●	✎ ✎		150	75		Large flower spikes

 planting ● *flowering*

Erythronium

Dog's tooth
violet *or* Trout lily
or Fawn lily
BULB

The erythroniums have two attributes to offer the gardener – pendent flowers with gracefully reflexed petals and attractively mottled foliage. Add to this that they love cool shade and you have a group of plants worthy of any shaded position in the garden.

The flowers have prominent stamens and nod gracefully on stems rising above the foliage. The flowers can be up to 7.5cm (3in) across in *Erythronium revolutum*, but on average they are 4–6cm (1½-2½in) across. They may be borne singly as in *E. dens-canis*, in groups of three or four, *E. revolutum* and *E. californicum*, or up to ten or a dozen per flowering stem in *E.* 'Pagoda' and *E. tuolumnense*.

The bulbs are hardy down to -15°C (5°F) and need to be planted in cool, shady positions. Plant in shady rock gardens and

soil	Erythronium prefers a well-drained but moisture-retentive, humus-rich soil
site	Provide these plants with a position that offers partial shade
planting	Plant bulbs 7.5cm (3in) deep and space roughly 10cm (4in) apart
general care	Plants must be kept cool when growing and ensure the bulbs are not baked by the sun when dormant in summer
pests & disease	Slugs may cause problems, but apart from this, plants are relatively trouble free from most pests and diseases

mixed borders where they are shaded by other plants, but they look their best in the dappled shade under trees or in woodland gardens. Growing them around other plants that shade the soil will help prevent the bulbs becoming baked in summer, which they hate.

Because they need plenty of moisture-retentive humus in the soil you should mulch around plants every year with leafmould, garden compost or similar to keep the humus levels topped up.

Plants are propagated by dividing established clumps as the leaves fade, and replanting the divisions immediately to prevent the bulbs drying out. As plants generally dislike disturbance only do this when absolutely necessary.

Erythronium 'Pagoda'

Erythronium revolutum

	SPRING	SUMMER	AUTUMN	WINTER	height (cm)	spread (cm)	flower colour	
Erythronium californicum	● ●		✂ ✂		30	15		The green foliage is mottled brown-green
E. californicum 'White Beauty'	● ●		✂ ✂		25	15		Larger flowers than E. californicum
E. dens-canis	● ●		✂ ✂		25	15		Foliage has purple-brown marbling
E. 'Pagoda'	● ●		✂ ✂		40	20		Foliage has bronze mottling
E. revolutum	● ●		✂ ✂		25	20		Foliage has brown mottling
E. tuolumnense	● ●		✂ ✂		30	20		Plain green foliage

E

Bulbs

✂ *planting*   ● *flowering*

Eucharis
Amazon lily

Although Amazon lilies have been grown since the mid-19th century, they have sadly never been that popular. Admittedly they are a bit fussy in their requirements, but the recent boom in conservatories and conservatory plants should hopefully see something of a revival with this plant.

The exotic white, funnel-shaped flowers of *Eucharis amazonica* resemble large Narcissus and are produced at the top of stout stems in groups of between four and eight. They are deliciously fragrant and can measure up to 7.5cm (3in) wide. The plants themselves can reach up to 60cm (24in) high. Although the main flowering period is in the summer, plants may flower again in autumn or winter if the conditions are correct.

After potting in mid- to late spring, keep the compost on the dry side until growth begins, then start to water more moderately, increasing the frequency of watering to keep the compost moist when the plants are in active growth. Reduce watering after flowering and increase again when new growth is produced.

The plants are not frost hardy and need a minimum temperature of 10°C (50°F). Unlike many other conservatory

soil	For best results, plant these in a loam-based compost with added sharp sand
site	Eucharis prefers a position in bright light, especially in direct sunlight
planting	Plant Amazon lilies with the tip of the bulb just above compost level
general care	Water well; feed weekly during active growth, then stop feeding and water enough to prevent wilting once flowers have faded
pests & disease	Red spider mite and aphids can be a problem, but otherwise fairly trouble free from pests and diseases

plants that do not like direct sunlight, Amazon lilies need plenty of light and revel in these conditions, although they may need to be protected from the strong midday sun at the height of summer. They also need a humid atmosphere, so mist the foliage regularly, however not when it is in direct sunlight.

Plants should be repotted every three to four years using a 12.5–15cm (5–6in) pot. Plants can be propagated by removing offsets when repotting. The offsets should be grown on at 15°C (60°F) until established.

Eucharis amazonica

Eucomis
Pineapple flower
or Pineapple lily
BULB

The pineapple flower or lily is an exotic looking plant which will bring a touch of beauty to gardens, conservatories and greenhouses in summer and early autumn. Small, starry flowers are packed densely around a robust stem, topped with a tuft of leafy bracts.

Eucomis autumnalis

Eucomis bicolor

Eucomis comosa

When the flowers fade they produce long-lasting seed pods and, as a result, stems can be cut for indoor decoration.

The dark green, strap-like leaves form a basal rosette around the flowering stems. The leaves of *Eucomis bicolor* have purple edges and the stems have purple flecks. The leaves and stems of *E. comosa* have purple spots.

Although pineapple lilies can be planted in the garden, the bulbs are not hardy and need to be lifted in the autumn and stored at a minimum temperature of 4–10°C (39–50°F). The best way to grow them is in pots on the patio or sunk in the garden as the pots can then be easily moved indoors over winter. They can also be grown in cool greenhouses and conservatories. Plant one bulb per 12.5cm (5in) pot or, for a more dramatic effect, plant three bulbs in a 25–30cm (10–12in) one. When in growth, plants need a minimum temperature of 10°C (50°F).

Once the foliage starts to die down keep the compost dry, only starting to water again when new growth starts in spring.

Plants are propagated by removing offsets when repotting in spring.

soil	For best results, plant in a loam-based compost or well-drained soil
site	Indoors, a position in bright light but out of direct sunlight; outside, place in a sunny position
planting	Plant with tip of the bulb slightly above the surface of the compost or 15cm (6in) deep in the garden
general care	Keep the compost or soil just moist and feed plants regularly when in active growth
pests & disease	Relatively trouble free. Pests and diseases do not usually cause any problems to this plant

	SPRING	SUMMER	AUTUMN	WINTER	height (cm)	spread (cm)	flower colour	
Eucomis autumnalis	planting	flowering	flowering		40	60		Flowers turn deeper green as they age
E. bicolor	planting	flowering			60	30		Flowers are purple tinged
E. comosa	planting	flowering			60	50		Flowers have a violet-purple centre
E. pallidiflora	planting	flowering			75	50		A relatively slow growing plant

planting · flowering

Freesia
CORM

Hailing from South Africa, freesias are valued for their spikes of usually strongly fragrant flowers that are perfect for bringing scent and colour to the house, as well as greenhouses and sheltered borders outside.

Freesias are not hardy and can either be grown indoors to flower in winter and spring or, by buying and planting prepared corms, planted outside in mid to late spring for flowers in summer. In very mild, frost-free areas un-prepared corms can be planted outside in late summer or early autumn but may need a thick mulch of bark or similar to protect them over winter.

For growing indoors, plant corms in pots in succession from late summer through the autumn and early winter if you want flowers over a long period. After planting keep the compost just moist until growth begins, gradually increasing the watering and then watering regularly when in growth. Feed with a liquid high potash fertilizer fortnightly once the flower buds start to form. The pots should be kept at 5°C (40°F) until seven leaves have been produced when they should be kept at around 10°C (50°F); above 15°C (55°F) will produce spindly plants and flowers that fade quickly.

Reduce watering and stop feeding as the foliage fades and keep the compost dry when the corms are dormant. Corms can be lifted in mid- or late summer and stored in dry compost somewhere, dry, cool and frost free.

Outdoors keep plants well watered and fed when in growth. Once the foliage has died back the corms can be lifted and stored, however prepared bulbs will not flower at the same time the following year and should either be discarded or re-planted in autumn – indoors in cold areas.

Although named cultivars are available, shops usually only sell mixes of single or double-flowered corms.

Propagate plants by removing offsets at lifting time.

soil	Freesias will thrive in any good, well-drained soil or compost
site	Outside, plant in a sheltered sunny position; indoors, site in plenty of indirect sunlight
planting	Plant corms 4cm (1⅛in) deep and space them roughly 5–7.5cm (2–3in) apart
general care	Plants may need some form of support as they can become top heavy and the flowering stems collapse with the weight
pests & disease	Red spider mite, aphids and dry rot can affect plants grown under glass, but outside they are relatively trouble free

Freesia 'Yellow Tree'

	SPRING			SUMMER			AUTUMN			WINTER			height (cm)	spread (cm)	flower colour
Freesia 'Amulet'													30	5	Double flowers
F. 'Aphrodite'													30	5	Double flowers
F. 'Beethoven'													30	5	Single flowers
F. 'Blue Heaven'													30	5	Single flowers
F. 'Escapade'													30	5	Single flowers
F. 'Floriade'													30	5	Double flowers
F. 'Marianne'													30	5	Double flowers
F. 'Miranda'													30	5	Single flowers
F. 'Yellow Tree'													30	5	Double flowers

 planting   flowering

Fritillaria
Fritillary
BULB

Fritillaries are a versatile and varied group of plants that have numerous uses in the garden. All have attractive bell-shaped flowers. Some of the species produce flower stems with solitary flowers, others produce several grouped together on tall stems – such as the crown imperials, *Fritillaria imperialis*.

The flower colour ranges from white through yellow and red to green and dark brown almost black, sometimes attractively chequered or striped.

They are all suitable for growing in herbaceous borders, light open garden or rock garden. The easiest to grow include *F. acmopetala*, *F. pallidiflora*, *F. meleagris*, *F. michailovskyi*, *F. persica* and *F. pyrenaica*. They thrive in soils that have adequate moisture in summer when the plants are growing and do not become baked dry in summer. *F. meleagris* is perfect for naturalizing in grass and on banks providing the above conditions can be met.

F. michailovskyi and *F. persica* benefit from being kept dry when the foliage dies down until early autumn so are best grown in pots in damp areas.

F. imperialis is a stately plant for borders producing a ring of large flowers on stout stems below a tuft of leafy bracts so that it resembles a pineapple. The bulbs are hollow-crowned and hold water so are best planted on their side otherwise they may rot. The flowers also smell foxy, so plant away from the house and sitting areas.

Many species are also perfectly suited to growing in pots on the patio or cold greenhouse where the flowers can be viewed close up and enjoyed even more.

Plants are propagated by removing offsets when lifting and dividing in autumn.

soil	Fritillaries will grow their best planted in any well-drained soil
site	Prefers to be sited in a position where there is sun or light shade
planting	Plant 10–15cm (4–6in) deep, *F. imperialis* 20cm (8in); 15cm (6in) apart, *F. imperialis* 45cm (18in)
general care	Ensure the soil is kept moist when growing. Remove the foliage once it has died down
pests & disease	Slugs, snails and scarlet lily beetle may be a problem. Grey mould can be a problem under glass

Fritillaria imperialis 'Rubra Maxima'

	SPRING	SUMMER	AUTUMN	WINTER	height (cm)	spread (cm)	flower colour	
Fritillaria acmopetala	● ●		planting		35	8		Flowers hang singly or in groups of two or three
F. imperialis 'Aureomarginata'	● ●		planting		125	30		Variegated foliage
F. imperialis 'Maxima Lutea'	● ●		planting		150	30		Flowers in groups up to six
F. imperialis 'Rubra Maxima'	● ●		planting		150	30		Flowers in groups up to six
F. meleagris	● ● ●		planting		25	8		Flowers chequered dark purple
F. meleagris alba	● ●		planting		25	8		Normally one flower per stem
F. michailovskyi	● ●		planting		15	8		Flowers in groups up to three
F. pallidiflora	● ●		planting		40	8		Blue-green foliage
F. persica 'Adiyaman'	● ●		planting		90	10		Flowers in groups up to two
F. pyrenaica	●		planting		40	10		Narrow, blue-green foliage
F. uva-vulpis	● ● ●		planting		25	10		Glossy foliage

 planting ● flowering

Galanthus
Snowdrop
BULB

Snowdrops are the one flowering bulb that just about everyone knows and looks forward to seeing as they so triumphantly mark winter and the beginning of spring. Snowdrops grow naturally in woodlands or cool mountain meadows.

All species of galanthus have white nodding flowers made up of six unequal petals. The longer outer ones are usually plain white, whereas the shorter inner ones form a cup and have distinctive green markings.

Plants normally have two narrow basal leaves that are short at flowering time and then extend afterwards. They need a position that is neither hot nor dry. The dappled shade produced by trees is the best position for them, although they also grow well beneath and around shrubs and herbaceous plants. These conditions are particularly important during their summer dormancy. *Galanthus nivalis* can also be naturalized in light grass.

They are not too fussy about soils types – including heavy clay – but if planting in light, sandy soils dig in plenty of humus at planting time. *G. elwesii* is best in dry, alkaline soils.

soil	Tolerates most soils, preferring a well-drained but humus-rich, moist soil
site	Prefers a position in light shade where it is neither too hot nor too dry
planting	Plant bulbs 10cm (4in deep) and space roughly 10cm (4in) apart
general care	Lift and divide congested plants in the green (while still in leaf) immediately after flowering
pests & disease	Eelworm, narcissus fly and grey mould can be a problem, but otherwise fairly trouble free from pests and diseases

The dried bulbs available in the autumn do not always grow away strongly so make sure you buy yours as early in the season as possible. Or, if possible, buy potted plants or plants lifted while still in leaf – or 'in the green' as it is referred to.

Although generally winter flowering, *G. reginae-olgae* is autumn flowering and is often still in flower in winter. It is best planted in a dry, sunny position.

Plants can be propagated by lifting clumps immediately after flowering, removing offsets and replanting immediately. Water well after transplanting.

Galanthus 'Magnet'

	SPRING	SUMMER	AUTUMN	WINTER	height (cm)	spread (cm)	flower colour	
Galanthus 'Atkinsii'			planting	flowering	20	8		Flowers up to 4cm long
G. elwesii			planting	flowering	20	8		Flowers up to 3cm long
G. 'Magnet'	flowering		planting	flowering	23	8		Flowers up to 3cm long
G. nivalis			planting	flowering	15	5		Flowers up to 2.5cm long
G. nivalis 'Flore Pleno'			planting	flowering	15	5		Double flowers
G. plicatus			planting	flowering	20	8		Flowers up to 2.5cm long
G. reginae-olgae subsp. *reginae-olgae*			planting / flowering	flowering	10	5		Flowers faintly scented
G. 'Sam Arnott'	flowering		planting	flowering	23	8		Large, almond-scented flowers
G. woronowii			planting	flowering	20	8		Small flowers with bright glossy green foliage

 planting ● *flowering*

Galtonia
Summer hyacinth
BULB

The summer hyacinth is a stately summer performer that looks elegant when planted in herbaceous and mixed borders. In late summer and early autumn the tall spires of up to 30 nodding, bell-shaped flowers up to 2.5cm (1in) long rise above the glossy, strap-like leaves.

The flowers open in succession and so provide a display over quite a long time; those of *Galtonia candicans* are also pleasantly fragrant. Galtonias are particularly useful for flowering above the faded foliage of earlier perennials.

They do not look as impressive when grown as individual plants, so plant bold groups of around ten bulbs.

Galtonias can also be grown as a cool greenhouse or conservatory plant. Plant the bulbs 10cm (4in) deep in pots in early autumn to have flowers in late spring or early summer.

The bulbs are hardy down to -10°C (14°F) providing they are given a thick mulch of leafmould or compost in autumn. In very cold or wet areas it may be better to also cover them with a cloche or, better still, lift the bulbs in late autumn and store them in a frost-free place in trays of peat or similar material throughout winter until it is time to replant in spring.

Plants can be propagated by lifting established clumps in spring and separating out young bulbs for growing on. However, plants dislike disturbance so it may be better to buy new bulbs or try to carefully remove bulbs around the edge of the clump while still in the ground.

Galtonia candicans

Galtonia viridiflora

soil	Galtonia needs to be planted in a well-drained, humus-rich soil
site	For best results, place these plants in a position where there is full sun
planting	Plant the bulbs 15cm (6in) deep and space them out roughly 30cm (12in) apart
general care	Cut back flower stems once the flowers have faded. Make sure the soil does not dry out when the plants are in leaf
pests & disease	Relatively trouble free. Pests and diseases do not usually cause any problems to this plant

	SPRING	SUMMER	AUTUMN	WINTER	height (cm)	spread (cm)	flower colour	
Galtonia candicans					100	30		Bright green foliage
G. viridiflora					75	30		Grey-green foliage

planting   flowering

Gladiolus

Sword lily
CORM

Valued for their large spikes of summer flowers in a wide range of bright, vivid colours, gladioli are perfect dot plants for borders or for bedding out in massed displays. Gladioli not only bring a splash of colour to beds and borders during summer, they are also grown for cut flowers for indoor decoration. And when the gladioli bug really bites, they are a marvellous sight when exhibited en masse or at flower shows.

Gladiolus 'Flevo Junior'

The large-flowered hybrids are the best known and most widely grown and produce the showiest flower spikes. Cultivars can reach a height of up to 1.8m (6ft), with flower spikes up to 50cm (20in) long and each flower can measure up to 17.5cm (7in) across. They can be divided into Giant, Large, Medium, Miniature and Small depending on their flower spike length and flower size.

Although the large-flowered hybrids are the commonest types, there are a couple of others that are generally shorter and with a more delicate appearance.

Gladiolus 'Drama'

The Primulinus Hybrids produce flowers that are up to 7.5cm (3in) across, the top petal is hooded and the flowers are loosely arranged on the stem. The flowers of the Butterfly Hybrids are up to 10cm (4in) across and closely packed on the flower stem. They have ruffled petals and usually very striking throats. The Nanus Hybrids are like small Primulinus Hybrids, growing up to 60cm (2ft) high with flowers up to 5cm (2in) across and often with frilled or ruffled petals. The final group are the species which are generally hardier than the others – usually surviving outside over winter, so they can be planted

Gladiolus 'Ivory Queen'

soil	Gladioli will perform at their best when planted in any well-drained soil
site	These plants prefer as warm and sunny a position as possible in the garden
planting	Plant 10–15cm (4–6in) deep; 12.5–20cm (5–8in) apart. Put corms on sharp sand to improve drainage
general care	Tall cultivars will need to be staked with a bamboo cane and the stems tied to the cane for support
pests & disease	Thrips, aphids and eelworms, scab and virus can be a problem on the plants. Mould can affect corms in storage

	SPRING	SUMMER	AUTUMN	WINTER	height (cm)	spread (cm)	flower colour	
G. callianthus		● ●			100	5	▢	Scented flowers with purple blotches
G. 'Comet'	● ●				75	8	▪	Nanus type
G. communis subsp. *byzantinus*	● ●				100	8	▨	Quite hardy
G. 'Drama'		● ●			170	10	▨	Large
G. 'Flevo Junior'		● ●			60	5	▪	Small
G. 'Georgette'		● ●			120	10	▪	Butterfly hybrid; flowers have yellow centres
G. 'Green Woodpecker'		● ●			150	10	▨	Medium
G. 'Ivory Queen'		● ● ●			150	10	▢	Large

🪏 *planting*   ● *flowering*

Gladiolus 'Sharkey'

Gladiolus 'Robinetta'

in autumn in mild areas, and flower in late spring to early summer. A number of excellent hybrids have been produced from some of the species. These more compact types are better choices for windy or exposed gardens as they rarely need staking and can be grown in containers.

There is one 'oddity' – *Gladiolus callianthus*, which you may find listed as *Acidanthera murielae*. This species produces spikes of up to 10 sweetly scented white flowers with a central purple blotch. This plant is not hardy and will need lifting in late autumn and the corms stored in a warm, dry place. In cold areas it may fail to flower outdoors and is then best grown in a cool greenhouse or conservatory.

Gladioli corms should be planted in spring and because the individual flower spikes do not last that long, it pays to plant the corms in succession at fortnightly intervals to extend the flowering period.

Plants need very little aftercare, but should be watered in periods of dry weather once the flower spikes appear. Be vigilant for thrips, which can cause damage to the flowers.

Although the corms can be left in the ground over winter in mild areas, it pays to lift them in mid-autumn before serious frosts threaten. Carefully remove the soil then place the corms in a warm place before storing in a cool but frost-free place until it is time to re-plant in spring.

Plants can be propagated by removing and storing cormlets at lifting time; they will usually take two to three years to reach flowering size.

Gladiolus 'The Bride'

	SPRING	SUMMER	AUTUMN	WINTER	height (cm)	spread (cm)	flower colour	
G. 'Leonore'	planting	flowering			110	10		Primulinus hybrid
G. murielae	planting	flowering			100	10		Moderately hardy
G. 'Nova Lux'	planting	flowering			100	10		Large
G. 'Nymph'	planting	flowering			70	8		Nanus type
G. papilio	planting	flowering	flowering		90	8		Moderately hardy
G. 'Peter Pears'	planting	flowering			100	8		Large
G. 'Robinetta'	planting	flowering			60	5		Recurvus hybrid; flowers have white markings
G. 'Royal Dutch'	planting	flowering			170	15		Large
G. 'Sharkey'	planting	flowering	flowering		150	10		Giant
G. 'The Bride'	planting/flowering				60	5		Colvillii hybrid
G. 'Trader Horn'	planting	flowering			100	8		Giant; flowers have white markings
G. tristis	planting/flowering				125	8		Flowers scented at night
G. 'White Friendship'	planting	flowering			100	8		Large

planting   flowering

Habranthus
BULB

This is an attractive plant that can be easily grown outside in mild areas, although it is usually best treated as an indoor plant for growing in a cool greenhouse or conservatory.

Habranthus produces dainty flowers on top of an upright stem, the flowers being held at a characteristic angle. Habranthus literally means dainty flower. It is a member of the Amaryllis family, although the flowers are nowhere near as large and impressive as hippeastrums; in fact, Habranthus is more like a crocus in appearance.

The foliage appears after the flowers and persists into late spring.

Although they can be grown outdoors at the base of a warm sunny wall in sheltered gardens that experience little or no frost, Habranthus are more reliable when grown in pots in a greenhouse or conservatory at a minimum temperature of 7°C (45°F). *Habranthus tubispathus* is more reliably hardy than *H. robustus*. Alternatively, pots can be moved outside during the summer but moved under cover again before the first autumn frost.

For growing in containers and pots, use a loam-based compost and plant firmly, keeping the neck and shoulders of the bulb above compost level. Allow the compost to remain only just moist until growth begins, when you can then start to water more freely to keep the compost moist. Begin to reduce watering once the foliage starts to fade, and make sure the compost is kept dry, but not bone dry, when the bulbs are dormant. You do not need to repot annually, because plants will flower better if kept slightly potbound.

Plants are propagated by lifting and dividing the clumps in autumn.

Habranthus robustus

Habranthus robustus

soil	Habranthus needs to be planted in a well-drained, humus-rich soil
site	For best results, place these plants in a sheltered position in the full sun
planting	Plant the bulbs 10cm (4in) deep and space them out roughly 15cm (6in) apart
general care	Feed Habranthus weekly when the flower spikes start to appear with a liquid fertilizer
pests & disease	Relatively trouble free. Pests and diseases do not usually cause any problems to this plant

	SPRING	SUMMER	AUTUMN	WINTER	height (cm)	spread (cm)	flower colour	
Habranthus robustus	🌱 🌱	● ● ●	●		30	10	▨	Flowers are up to 7.5cm long
H. tubispathus	🌱 🌱	● ●			20	10	▥	Flowers are 2.5cm long

 planting   ● flowering

Haemanthus

Blood lily *or*
Shaving brush

BULB

The unusual, brush-like central boss of stamens surrounded by petal-like bracts give rise to this plant's common name of shaving brush. They make unusual and attractive houseplants and conservatory plants.

The foliage can either be evergreen, as in *Haemanthus albiflos*, or deciduous as in *H. coccineus*, in which case it is produced after the flowers. The evergreen *H. albiflos* is therefore the one to grow as a houseplant. The foliage of *H. coccineus* is also marked with deep red-purple and the flower stems have attractive red spots.

Haemanthus prefers to be under-potted, so always use as small a pot as possible. They hate root disturbance and may remain in the same pot for a number of years. Only repot when absolutely necessary and when growth restarts in spring.

Plants need a minimum temperature of 10°C (50°F) and bright but diffused light. Move into part shade when the flower buds begin to colour to preserve the colour and prolong the flowering period. Those grown as houseplants can tolerate lower temperatures providing they are grown in good light.

As the leaves of deciduous plants start to yellow, stop watering until growth starts again. Those with evergreen leaves will need

soil	Pot up using a loam-based compost with added grit in a pot twice the diameter of the bulb
site	Needs a position in good light but out of direct sunlight to perform at its best
planting	Plant with the tip of the bulb just above the surface of the compost; one bulb per pot
general care	Water and feed with a liquid fertilizer regularly when in growth, but keep them dry at other times
pests & disease	Mealy bug may be a problem from time to time, but otherwise they are rarely troubled by pests and diseases

the compost to be kept dry but not bone dry during their dormant period.

Plants can be propagated by removing offsets when growth begins in spring. Carefully remove them, pot up and keep in a covered propagator or similar.

Haemanthus coccineus

	SPRING	SUMMER	AUTUMN	WINTER	height (cm)	spread (cm)	flower colour
Haemanthus albiflos	🌱 🌱	● ●			30	30	☐ Foliage is evergreen
H. coccineus	🌱 🌱	● ●			30	30	▣ Foliage is deciduous

🌱 *planting*   ✹ *flowering*

Hedychium

Ginger lily *or*
Garland flower

RHIZOME

The ginger lilies were popular back in the mid-19th century and, thanks to the increased popularity of outdoor exotics, are once again back in favour with modern gardeners. They are half hardy and should be treated as summer bedding plants.

Their large foliage and imposing flower spikes make them ideal choices as specimen or dot plants adding height to herbaceous and summer borders. They can also be grown in large containers on patios, or in warm greenhouses and conservatories where they can flower any time between late spring and autumn.

Hedychium gardnerianum

The rhizomes are bought from late winter to early spring. Although they can be planted directly outside in late spring it is much better to start them into growth planted in pots in spring with gentle heat. This produces good sized plants for planting outside in late spring or early summer – after the fear of frosts has passed.

Although one or two species can survive a degree or two of frost and could be left outside in winter if covered with a thick mulch, it is better to lift plants in late autumn and overwinter them in a frost-free place, or grow them in pots.

Cut down the stems to ground level, then carefully lift the rhizomes, remove any soil or compost and trim away any dead growth. Then store in slightly moist compost or sand and keep the rhizomes in a frost-free place. Check the rhizomes periodically to ensure they do not shrivel and dry out, nor become too damp, which can encourage rotting.

Plants can be propagated by dividing the rhizomes before potting up or planting outside in spring.

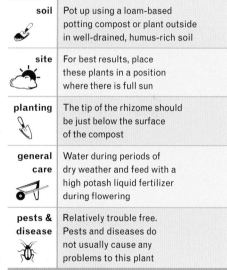

soil	Pot up using a loam-based potting compost or plant outside in well-drained, humus-rich soil
site	For best results, place these plants in a position where there is full sun
planting	The tip of the rhizome should be just below the surface of the compost
general care	Water during periods of dry weather and feed with a high potash liquid fertilizer during flowering
pests & disease	Relatively trouble free. Pests and diseases do not usually cause any problems to this plant

Bulbs

	SPRING	SUMMER	AUTUMN	WINTER	height (cm)	spread (cm)	flower colour	
Hedychium coccineum	potting up	planting, flowering	flowering		200	100	■	Flowers on 30cm long spikes
H. coronarium	potting up	planting, flowering	flowering		240	100	□	Flowers on 30cm long spikes
H. densiflorum	potting up	planting, flowering	flowering		300	100	▦	Flowers on 20cm long spikes
H. gardnerianum	potting up	planting, flowering	flowering		150	100	▨	Flowers on 35cm long spikes
H. greenei	potting up	planting, flowering	flowering		180	100	■	Flowers on 15cm long spikes
H. spicatum	potting up	planting, flowering	flowering		150	60	□	Flowers on 20cm long spikes

 potting up   *planting*   *flowering*

Hermodactylus

Widow iris

TUBER

Aptly named thanks to its yellowish green and dark brown or blackish flowers, the widow iris is an attractive but curious plant for early and mid-spring colour. There is just one species in this genus, *Hermodactylus tuberosus*, which is closely related to Iris and is often listed as *Iris tuberosa*.

The scented flowers are borne singly on erect stems and emerge from the slender, grass-like leaves in early to mid-spring, although plants may start to flower in late winter in favourable years.

Hermodactylus needs as warm a position as possible, as the dormant tubers need plenty of summer sun in order to flower well the following year. Plant from late summer to mid-autumn. It prefers a limey soil, so add garden lime at planting time if your soil is acidic (pH 6.5 or lower) in nature.

The best places to plant Hermodactylus are at the edge of a sunny border, at the base of a sunny wall, in raised beds or on a rock garden where the tubers will receive plenty of sunlight. Plants need little in

soil	Hermodactylus needs to be planted in well-drained, limey to neutral soil
site	For best results, place these plants in a warm position where there is full sun
planting	Plant the tubers 5cm (2in) deep and space them roughly 10cm (4in) apart
general care	Care and maintenance is relatively low as these plants are easy to cultivate. Remove flowerheads after flowering
pests & disease	Slugs and aphids may be a problem, but otherwise relatively free from pests and diseases

Hermodactylus tuberosus

the way of care and attention, and can be left to their own devices to build up large, imposing clumps, 30cm (12in) high.

Although hardy to -15°C (5°F), it can be grown in pots of gritty compost in a cold greenhouse where the flowers can be enjoyed close up. This is certainly more appropriate in regions where cold and very wet spring weather can spoil the flowers.

Plants can be propagated by dividing and replanting the tubers in late summer.

Hippeastrum

Amaryllis
BULB

The indoor amaryllis is a huge hit with everyone who needs some winter cheer inside the house. The large, trumpet-shaped flowers of modern hybrids can be up to 25cm (10in) across and produced in clusters of up to six flowers.

Hippeastrums are traditionally bought in autumn and winter to be used as Christmas houseplants; plants will normally flower between one to three months after planting depending on conditions. However, later potting will produce flowers in spring, so for extended colour pot up bulbs over several weeks. The plants need a minimum temperature of 13°C (55°F).

If you want to ensure the bulbs flower the following year, it is essential to keep the foliage healthy and growing for as long as possible after flowering so they build up the bulb's strength. Sadly, because the foliage can get in the way after flowering, many people cut off the leaves – and are then disappointed when plants refuse to flower again!

After potting up, water the compost sparingly at first but increase watering as the foliage develops. Keep the compost moist when the leaves are green but when it starts to turn yellow, reduce watering and stop altogether when it is dead. Remove the old foliage and keep the bulb dormant until new foliage appears.

Plants prefer to be kept potbound, so only repot when the bulb outgrows the pot. Otherwise just scrape off any loose compost and replace with fresh when new growth appears.

Plants are propagated by removing offsets in spring.

soil	Plant in any good potting compost in a pot 5cm (2in) wider than the bulb
site	For best results, place these plants in a brightly lit position
planting	Plant with half the bulb exposed above the compost; plant one bulb per pot
general care	Feed with a liquid fertilizer every seven to 10 days when in growth. Remove the faded flowers as soon as they fade
pests & disease	Mealy bug, red spider mite, thrips and virus can all cause problems for Hippeastrum

Hippeastrum papilio

	SPRING	SUMMER	AUTUMN	WINTER	height (cm)	spread (cm)	flower colour	
Hippeastrum 'Apple Blossom'	flowering		planting	planting	50	30		Flowers streaked and tipped pink
H. 'Belinda'	flowering		planting	planting	60	30		Bright red flowers
H. 'Bestseller'	flowering		planting	planting	50	30		Short stemmed
H. 'Orange Souvereign'	flowering		planting	planting	50	30		Long-lasting flowers
H. papilio	flowering		planting	planting	40	25		Flowers marked dark red
H. 'Picotee'	flowering		planting	planting	50	30		Flowers have a red margin
H. 'Red Lion'	flowering		planting	planting	50	30		Flowers have yellow anthers
H. 'Star of Holland'	flowering		planting	planting	60	30		Flowers have a white throat
H. 'Yellow Pioneer'	flowering		planting	planting	60	30		Flowers paler in strong sunlight

 planting ⚬ flowering

Homeria
CORM

Being native of sandy habitats in South Africa, Homeria needs a warm, sunny position and well-drained soil to thrive. It bears a succession of lovely cup-shaped or starry flowers over a long period, especially if planted in both spring and autumn.

Although frost tender, Homeria can be grown outdoors in areas where winter temperatures do not fall much below -5°C (23°F) providing plants are given a deep mulch in winter to protect the corms. However, to be on the safe side it is usually a better idea to lift the corms in autumn and store them in a cool, but frost-free, dry place. Unless the soil is very well drained, plant the corms on a layer of sharp sand to ensure good drainage and prevent rotting.

Corms can be planted outside in spring to produce summer flowers, or an alternative use is to plant up in pots in autumn and keep them in a greenhouse or conservatory for flowers in spring.

When growing in pots, plant five corms together in gritty compost. Containers can be stood outside on a sunny patio after the fear of frosts has passed. Indoors plants need plenty of ventilation to prevent temperatures getting too high and a minimum temperature of 5–7°C (40–45°F). Water copiously when in growth but start to allow the compost to dry off when the flowers have finished flowering. Repot the corms in autumn.

Plants are propagated by dividing the clumps of established plants or removing the offsets.

soil	Plant in any good potting compost or in well-drained, humus-rich soil
site	Needs a brightly lit position indoors or an outdoor site in the full sun
planting	Plant 2.5cm (1in) deep in pots or 7.5cm (3in) outside; six to a 12.5–15cm pot or 7.5cm apart outdoors
general care	Care and maintenance is fairly low for this plant. Water and feed regularly when plants are growing
pests & disease	Relatively trouble free. Pests and diseases do not usually cause any problems to this plant

Homeria flaccida

	SPRING	SUMMER	AUTUMN	WINTER	height (cm)	spread (cm)	flower colour	
Homeria flaccida	●●●	●●●	⚘⚘		60	10		Flowers have peach or red markings
H. ochroleuca	●●●	●●●	⚘⚘		80	10		Flowers have a musky scent and often an orange centre

 planting ● flowering

Hyacinthoides
Bluebell
BULB

The bluebell is a common sight in European woodlands, where the large carpets of blue flowers in spring are worth searching out. Over the years the bluebells have been variously named, being regarded as both Endymion and Scilla.

Hyacinthoides italica

Hyacinthoides non-scripta

Whatever their name, bluebells are hardy and can be relied upon to produce their spikes of up to 20 2cm (¾in) drooping bells whatever the weather. In *Hyacinthoides non-scripta* the flowers are arranged on just one side of the flower spike.

In fact, bluebells grow so readily, produce plenty of seed and spread so quickly they can become a nuisance. The Spanish bluebell, *H. hispanica*, is even more vigorous than the British *H. non-scripta* and hybrids between the two are out-competing the latter and causing their decline both in the wild and in gardens.

Bluebells can be planted in wildflower gardens or naturalized in grass, but are best in woodland, around trees or underneath shrubs where the cool, semi-shaded conditions intensifies the flower colour and prevents it from becoming bleached. When planted in large drifts the heady fragrance of the flowers of *H. non-scripta* becomes almost hypnotic. The strap-like, fleshy leaves can help provide ground cover.

Once planted, bulbs can be left to their own devices. But it is a good idea to remove the faded flower spikes before they set seed to prevent the plants self-seeding and becoming invasive.

Plants are propagated by dividing congested clumps in late summer.

soil	Hyacinthoides will do well in any humus-rich, moist soil
site	For best results, find a position where there is either sun or partial shade
planting	Plant the bulbs 7.5cm (3in) deep and space them out 10–15cm (4–6in) apart
general care	Bluebells are extremely easy to grow and need very little care and attention as plants tend to take care of themselves
pests & disease	Relatively trouble free. Pests and diseases do not usually cause any problems to this plant

	SPRING	SUMMER	AUTUMN	WINTER	height (cm)	spread (cm)	flower colour	
Hyacinthoides hispanica	● ●		🌱 🌱		45	15		Pink and white-flowered forms available
H. italica	● ●		🌱 🌱		20	15		Flowers densely packed together
H. non-scripta	● ●		🌱 🌱		30	30		Flowers scented. White-flowered form available

 planting   ● flowering

Hyacinthus

Hyacinth

<small>BULB</small>

Although hyacinths make excellent garden plants, they are more commonly grown indoors for winter or early spring displays on windowsills, table tops or just about anywhere else their colourful, fragrant flowers can be enjoyed.

The plants of the Dutch hyacinth, *Hyacinthus orientalis* – with their erect flowerheads densely packed with up to 60 flowers and fleshy, strap-like foliage – can look perfect for up to three weeks in the right conditions. They are excellent for growing in containers outside – but ensure the compost does not get frosted right through – in informal borders and more formal bedding schemes.

Providing the bulbs were planted in good soil with plenty of added humus they can be left in the ground all year. However, the display in the subsequent years may not be as good and when used in formal bedding schemes this may be a disadvantage. Instead, it may be a better idea to let the foliage die down, then lift the bulbs

soil	Hyacinths need to be planted in a humus-rich soil for best results
site	Plants can be grown in light shade but prefer to be in the sun
planting	Plant the bulbs 10–12.5cm (4–5in) deep and space roughly 15–20cm (6–8in) apart
general care	Feed the plants well during and after flowering with a liquid fertilizer. Otherwise, fairly easy to grow
pests & disease	Aphids, slugs, eelworm and narcissus fly may be a problem. Bulbs may be attacked by bulb rot and grey mould

Hyacinthus orientalis 'Blue Jacket'

Hyacinthus orientalis 'Gipsy Queen'

Hyacinthus orientalis 'Amethyst'

and store them in dry compost in a cool, dry place until it is time to replant in autumn. Where the ground is needed for summer displays you can lift the bulbs after flowering and heel them in to another patch of soil until the foliage dies down, then lift and store them.

Bulbs can also be planted singly in 10–12.5cm (4–5in) pots or even suspended at water level in glass jars or grouped together in larger bowls for indoor displays during late winter and early spring. For mid-winter displays indoors you will have to buy specially prepared bulbs and plant them in late summer or early autumn as they need up to 10 weeks in a cool, dark conditions to flower properly (see page 17 for details).

After flowering these can be planted out in the garden in spring after hardening off because they will not flower again at the same time and in subsequent years the displays are not as prominent.

Multiflora hyacinths are also available. These have been treated to produce several smaller flower spikes instead of one dense spike and can be grown inside or out.

They are usually only sold by colour. You may also find the smaller, looser-flowered Roman hyacinths derived from *H. orientalis* var. *albulus*. These are for indoor culture only and are available in white, pink or blue.

Be careful when handling the bulbs as dust from their skins can cause irritation.

Plants are propagated by a method called scoring (see page 20 for details). Or you can remove offsets at lifting time.

Hyacinthus orientalis 'Pink Pearl'

	SPRING	SUMMER	AUTUMN	WINTER	height (cm)	spread (cm)	flower colour	
Hyacinthus orientalis 'Amethyst'	● ●		✂ ✂		25	8		Late flowering
H. orientalis 'Anna Marie'	● ●		✂ ✂		25	8		Early flowering
H. orientalis 'Blue Jacket'	● ●		✂ ✂		25	8		Mid-season flowering
H. orientalis 'Borah'	● ●		✂ ✂		25	8		Early flowering
H. orientalis 'Carnegie'	● ●		✂ ✂		25	8		Late flowering
H. orientalis 'City of Haarlem'	● ●		✂ ✂		25	8		Late flowering
H. orientalis 'Delft Blue'	● ●		✂ ✂		25	8		Early flowering
H. orientalis 'Gipsy Queen'	● ●		✂ ✂		25	8		Mid-season flowering
H. orientalis 'Hollyhock'	● ●		✂ ✂		25	8		Late flowering
H. orientalis 'Jan Bos'	● ●		✂ ✂		25	8		Early flowering
H. orientalis 'L'Innocence'	● ●		✂ ✂		25	8		Early flowering
H. orientalis 'Ostara'	● ●		✂ ✂		25	8		Early flowering
H. orientalis 'Pink Pearl'	● ●		✂ ✂		25	8		Early flowering

✂ planting   ● flowering

Hymenocallis

Spider lily

Bulb

Looking more like a daffodil than a lily, Hymenocallis gets its common name from the ring of narrow reflexed petals that stick out at the base of the trumpet-shaped flower cup – although there are only six of them!

The fragrant flowers are produced at the top of leafless stems in groups of two to five above the narrow, dark green, strap-like leaves.

Plants are not hardy and need a minimum temperature of 13°C (55°F). Because of this they are most often grown in pots as a houseplant, in a greenhouse or conservatory or moved onto a warm patio when in flower, but they can also be grown in the ground in a warm, sheltered, sunny position.

soil	Plant in a loam-based compost indoors or well-drained, humus-rich soil outside
site	Good light, but away from direct sunlight indoors or a sheltered, sunny position outside
planting	Plant with the tip of bulb above the compost or 12.5cm (5in) deep in the garden
general care	Water regularly when in leaf, and feed with a liquid fertilizer once flower buds appear and until the foliage starts to yellow
pests & disease	Aphids may be a problem, but otherwise spider lilies are relatively free from pests and diseases

Outside the bulbs are planted in early summer for flowers in late summer, whereas inside they are planted in early spring for summer flowers. When grown outside bulbs can be left in the ground in frost-free gardens in winter protected with a thick mulch, but to ensure survival they are best lifted in autumn and stored in a dry, frost-free place.

When growing in pots, water the compost sparingly until the foliage appears, then water and feed regularly. Stop watering when the leaves begin to wither in autumn and leave the bulbs dormant in the pots over winter. Bulbs will flower more prolifically if kept potbound, but repot them every three years. Put one bulb in a 10cm (4in) pot or three bulbs per 30cm (12in) pot, or 30cm (12in) apart in the garden.

Plants are propagated by removing offsets when repotting or replanting.

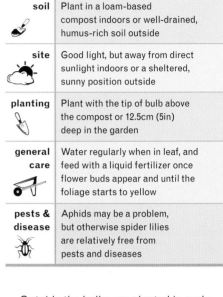

Hymenocallis x festalis

	SPRING	SUMMER	AUTUMN	WINTER	height (cm)	spread (cm)	flower colour	
Hymenocallis x festalis	🌱	●•●●●			80	40	☐	Flowers up to 20cm (8in) across
H. 'Sulphur Queen'	🌱	●•●●●			60	40	▦	Flowers have green stripes

🌱 planting　　● flowering

H

Bulbs

Ipheion

Spring starflower
BULB

Ipheions are dainty, spring-flowering plants that look their best when they have been allowed to establish for a few years and produce large clumps that will then continue to flower profusely.

The starry flowers up to 4cm (1½in) across have a pleasant scent and are produced singly on thin stems. They open among dense clumps of narrow, grassy, arching foliage that smells of garlic when crushed. Plants can be shy to flower in their first year or two but soon get into flowering mode if left alone.

The bulbs are best planted at the base of a wall or on a warm rockery, especially *Ipheion* 'Rolf Fiedler', which is not completely hardy when grown in cold conditions combined with wet soil. Plants will also appreciate some protection from the sun during the hottest part of the day in summer. Ipheions can also be grown in pots in a cold greenhouse or conservatory, which especially suits 'Rolf Fiedler'.

Although *I. uniflorum* and cultivars are hardy down to -10°C (14°F), you should mulch the soil in winter when prolonged frosts are expected.

Plants can be propagated by lifting and dividing clumps in late summer or autumn. Replant the bulbs immediately.

soil	Relatively unfussy, grows best planted in any well-drained soil
site	Ipheion requires a sheltered, sunny or very lightly shaded position
planting	Plant the bulbs 5cm (2in) deep and space them 10cm (4in) apart
general care	Plants prefer to be crowded together and left relatively undisturbed to build up a good-sized colony
pests & disease	Slugs and snails may be a problem, but otherwise relatively free from pests and diseases

Ipheion uniflorum 'Froyle Mill'

	SPRING	SUMMER	AUTUMN	WINTER	height (cm)	spread (cm)	flower colour	
Ipheion 'Alberto Castillo'	● ● ●		✄ ✄		15	8		Large flowers
I. 'Rolf Fiedler'	● ● ●		✄ ✄		15	8		Slightly tender
I. uniflorum	● ● ●		✄ ✄		15	8		Flowers tinged blue or violet
I. uniflorum 'Froyle Mill'	● ● ●		✄ ✄		15	8		Large flowers
I. uniflorum 'Wisley Blue'	● ● ●		✄ ✄		15	8		Flowers have a darker midrib

 planting   *flowering*

Iris
Bulb

Although the taller summer-flowering flag irises are the most showy of this genus, those that produce bulbs and mostly flower in late winter and spring are essential garden plants. There are three main types – the Reticulata group, the Xiphium group, which includes the popular summer-flowering Dutch irises, and the Juno group.

Iris 'Joyce'

The Reticulata group is made up of hardy species that flower from late winter with flowers measuring up to 7.5cm (3in) wide. They make excellent rock garden plants and for growing at the front of borders and beds.

The reticulatas are reliable and easy to care for, although *Iris danfordiae* has an annoying habit of splitting into several bulblets after flowering which can take two to four years to reach flowering size. All reticulatas benefit from three feeds at monthly intervals with a liquid fertilizer after flowering, and feeding the soil with a high nitrogen granular fertilizer in autumn.

The reticulatas can also be grown as indoor pot plants – planting six bulbs in a 12.5–15cm (5–6in) pot – and will flower in mid- to late winter. Do not bring plants into warm rooms until the flower buds show colour otherwise they will dry out and fail to open.

Plants are propagated by lifting the clumps and dividing them. Only do this when absolutely necessary because they dislike disturbance and should be left for four to five years at least.

The Xiphium group consists of the Dutch, Spanish and English irises, although it is only the first mentioned that are grown very often. They all flower in summer, the Dutch irises being the first to do so,

	SPRING	SUMMER	AUTUMN	WINTER	height (cm)	spread (cm)	flower colour	
Iris 'Bronze Perfection'		●	planting		60	30		Dutch
I. bucharica	● ●		planting		45	15		Juno. Flowers are scented
I. 'Cantab'	●		planting	●	15	5		Reticulata
I. danfordiae	●		planting	●	10	5		Reticulata
I. 'George'	●		planting	●	15	10		Reticulata. Larger flowers
I. 'Harmony'			planting	●	15	5		Reticulata
I. histrioides 'Major'	●		planting		15	7.5		Reticulata. Larger flowers
I. 'Joyce'	●		planting	●	12.5	7.5		Reticulata
I. 'J S Dijt'	●	●	planting	●	15	5		Reticulata
I. 'Katharine Hodgkin'	●		planting	●	12.5	7.5		Reticulata. Larger flowers

planting ● flowering

Iris 'Pauline'

soil	All irises prefer a well-drained, slightly alkaline, light soil
site	For best results, place these plants in a position where there is full sun
planting	Reticulata: 10cm deep and apart; Juno: 5–7.5cm deep, 15–23cm apart; Xiphium: 10–15cm deep, 15cm apart
general care	Not much in the way of general care. Keep the foliage growing for as long as possible by regular feeding
pests & disease	Aphids, eelworm, narcissus fly and bulb rot may be a problem, but otherwise fairly trouble free

producing flowers that are up to 12.5cm (5in) in diameter.

The Dutch irises need a position in rich soil in full sun and winter protection with a cloche or similar covering is worthwhile during hard winters, which may damage the overwintering foliage.

They can also be grown in pots for indoor flowering but should be kept in a cool greenhouse or similar until the flower buds show colour, otherwise they will dry out and fail to open. They make good cut flowers, but the bulbs may take a while to recover after the first flower stems have been cut.

Spanish irises need a warmer and drier position than the Dutch ones and the bulbs should be lifted when the foliage has died down, to assist bulb ripening, and then replanted in autumn. The English irises need rich soil and damp conditions.

All members of the Xiphium group are propagated by dividing the clumps after the foliage has died down.

The final selection, the Juno group, are not commonly grown. They need a position in the garden where shrubs or trees will shelter the plants and keep them as dry as possible in summer.

	SPRING	SUMMER	AUTUMN	WINTER	height (cm)	spread (cm)	flower colour	
I. magnifica	● ●		✏ ✏		60	15		Juno. Large flowers
I. 'Pauline'	●		✏ ✏	●	12.5	7.5		Reticulata
I. 'Purple Sensation'		●	✏ ✏		60	30		Dutch
I. reticulata	●		✏ ✏	●	15	5		Reticulata.
I. 'Romano'		●	✏ ✏		60	30		Dutch
I. 'Royal Yellow'		●	✏ ✏		60	30		Dutch
I. 'Symphony'		●	✏ ✏		60	30		Dutch
I. 'White Excelsior'		●	✏ ✏		60	30		Dutch. Petals with yellow blotches
I. winogradowii	● ●		✏ ✏		12.5	7.5		Reticulata

 ✏ planting ● flowering

Ixia

Corn lily *or*
Wand flower
CORM

Ixia maculata

The half-hardy South African ixias produce lots of attractive, starry flowers and are best grown in a cold or cool greenhouse or conservatory where their magnificent blooms will help bring a bright splash of colour to any plant collection.

The wiry stems produce dense clusters of around 20 flattish or bowl-shaped flowers up to 5cm (2in) across above narrow, sword-shaped leaves. The flowers tend to close on dull days.

Apart from the species listed, a number of brightly coloured named cultivars, ranging from white, through yellow to pink and red are offered by specialist growers, but these are usually sold as Mixed Hybrids in garden centres and shops.

Ixias can be grown outside in areas where the temperature seldom falls below freezing, but will need mulching with bark or leafmould. Plant in early spring and, for best

soil	Plant in either a loam-free compost indoors or good well-drained soil outside
site	Place in good light indoors, or a warm, sheltered, sunny position outside
planting	Plant 5cm deep in pots or 7.5cm deep in the garden; six to eight per pot or 9cm apart in the soil
general care	Keep plants reasonably well watered when in growth, but stop watering as the foliage starts to wither
pests & disease	Slugs and snails may be a problem, but otherwise relatively free from pests and diseases

results, lift in late summer to early autumn when the foliage dies down, and store the corms in a cool, dry place.

In other areas they are best grown as pot plants either moved to a warm, sunny patio when in flower or kept permanently in greenhouses and conservatories. For these situations they can be planted in autumn for spring and early summer flowers or in spring for flowers in late summer. Keep the compost fairly dry until growth starts, then water more frequently when in growth. Feed regularly with a liquid fertilizer when in growth. Stop watering when the foliage starts to die down and keep the compost dry until growth starts again. The flowers can be cut for indoor decoration.

Plants can be propagated by removing offsets in autumn; they usually take two years to flower.

Ixia paniculata

	SPRING	SUMMER	AUTUMN	WINTER	height (cm)	spread (cm)	flower colour
Ixia maculata					45	10	Flowers have yellow or orange central star
I. paniculata					60	10	Flowers tinged pink or red
I. viridiflora					60	10	Flowers have purple or red central blotch

planting   flowering

Ixiolirion
BULB

Ixiolirion is grown for its delicate-looking, funnel-shaped flowers that open into 5cm (2in) wide stars, mainly in late spring and early summer. It is not grown as commonly as perhaps it should be since bulbs are commonly available and relatively inexpensive.

Ixiolirion is hardy down to -15°C (5°F) but should be planted in a warm position, sheltered from cold winds, where the bulbs can be baked in summer to ripen and protected from excessive winter wet. This makes it especially useful for rock gardens, sunny raised beds and similar positions. The flowers look their best when set off by grey-leaved plants, such as Artemisia (wormwood), Lavandula (lavender) and Nepeta (catmint).

A winter mulch of bark or leafmould will help give extra protection to the bulbs and in very wet weather cover with an open-ended cloche or a suspended sheet of glass or plastic.

Or, if you prefer, plants can be grown in pots of loam-based compost in a cool greenhouse or conservatory. Keep the compost fairly dry until growth starts, then water frequently and feed with a liquid fertilizer every ten to 14 days when in growth. Stop watering when the foliage starts to die down and keep the pots in a sunny position and the compost dry until growth starts again. The cut flowers last well in water and are useful for indoor decoration.

Plants are propagated by lifting and removing offsets in autumn.

Ixiolirion tataricum

soil	Ixiolirion needs to be planted in any well-drained, light soil
site	For best results, a sheltered, sunny position is required
planting	Plant the bulbs 10cm (4in) deep and space them roughly 15cm (6in) apart
general care	Care and maintenance is fairly low for this plant. They are easy to care for given the correct conditions
pests & disease	Relatively trouble free. Pests and diseases do not usually cause any problems to this plant

	SPRING	SUMMER	AUTUMN	WINTER	height (cm)	spread (cm)	flower colour	
Ixiolirion tataricum	● ●	● ●	✎ ✎		45	10		Flowers have darker stripes
I. tataricum Ledebourii Group	● ●	● ●	✎ ✎		40	10		Flowers slightly earlier

 planting   *flowering*

Lachenalia

Cape cowslip
BULB

As their common name suggests, lachenalias hail from South Africa and are grown as indoor plants where their spikes of 2.5cm (1in) long waxy, pendulous tubular flowers can be produced for up to eight weeks.

Thankfully, lachenalias are becoming more popular as gardeners are increasing their search for both conservatory and greenhouse plants. The fact that they flower in winter and early spring adds to their interest, as does the foliage, which often has attractive dark blotches and markings.

After planting up the bulbs keep the pots in a well-ventilated greenhouse or conservatory at a temperature of 10–13°C (50–55°F) and in good light. Plants grown from bulbs potted in August and kept at 15–18°C (60–65°F) will flower for longer. Give the compost a good soaking after planting but then

Lachenalia aloides (syn. *L. tricolor*)

soil	Unfussy, as long as it is planted in a good potting compost
site	Needs a brightly lit position with some direct sunlight
planting	Plant with tip of bulb just below surface of the compost; plant five bulbs per 12.5cm (5in) pot
general care	Fairly easy care and maintenance. Keep the compost moist when plants are in growth
pests & disease	Relatively trouble free. Pests and diseases do not usually cause any problems to this plant

withhold water until new growth appears. Water moderately until the plants are in full growth and then water regularly, and feed every fortnight with a liquid fertilizer when in growth.

Plants can be brought into cool rooms in the house when in flower but ensure they receive plenty of light.

When the flowers have faded reduce watering until the foliage starts to turn yellow and then stop watering and allow the bulbs to dry off. They can be kept in the pots until it is time to repot them in fresh compost for the next flowering period.

Plants are propagated by removing offsets at planting time and will reach flowering size within two years.

Lachenalia aloides var. *aurea*

	SPRING	SUMMER	AUTUMN	WINTER	height (cm)	spread (cm)	flower colour	
Lachenalia aloides (syn. *L. tricolor*)	● ●	🖌 🖌		● ●	30	15		Flowers tinged with green and red
L. aloides var. aurea	●	🖌 🖌		● ●	30	15		Flowers without markings
L. aloides var. quadricolor	●	🖌 🖌		● ●	30	15		Flowers red when in bud
L. bulbifera	● ●	🖌 🖌		● ●	30	20		Flowers have purple or dark red markings
L. contaminata	● ●	🖌 🖌		●	25	15		Flowers have dark maroon tips
L. viridiflora	●	🖌 🖌		● ●	20	15		Flowers often have white tips

 🖌 planting ● flowering

Bulbs

Leucojum
Snowflake

Often confused with snowdrops, snowflakes are grown for their more rounded flowers, with all six petals the same length, which are produced in spring. The other distinguishing factor is that the white flowers often have yellow or green spots at the tips of the petals, and each stem may bear one or up to seven flowers, as in the case of *Leucojum aestivum*.

Leucojum vernum

Leucojum aestivum 'Gravetye Giant'

Positioning in the garden will depend on which species you are growing, as the plants in this genus come from a variety of natural habitats.

L. aestivum and *L. vernum* are best suited for naturalizing in moist soil in grass or for moist pockets on rock gardens. *L. aestivum* thrives in moist, heavy soil, is tolerant of waterlogged conditions and looks good when planted next to ponds and streams.

L. autumnale prefers warm, sunny positions and is an excellent choice for edging to borders and paths and growing on sunny rockeries. It is the least demanding to grow providing it is given well-drained conditions.

L. nicaeense similarly needs warmth and good drainage. For this reason it is also a good choice for growing in pots in a cold greenhouse where the flowers can be enjoyed close up, and where its need for hot dry dormant conditions and protection from winter wet can easily be achieved.

Plants are propagated by dividing clumps in spring or autumn, after flowering. But leucojums often take a while to become established and once they are the bulbs are best left undisturbed, so only divide the clumps when absolutely necessary.

Leucojum aestivum

soil	Generally requires any good, humus-rich, moisture-retentive soil	
site	Will grow in both sun or light shade, depending on species	
planting	Plant 5–10cm deep: *L. aestivum* 15cm apart; *L. autumnale*, *L. nicaeense*, *L. vernum* 5cm apart	
general care	Remove faded flowerheads and allow the foliage to die back naturally before removing it	
pests & disease	Relatively trouble free. Pests and diseases do not usually cause any problems to this plant	

	SPRING	SUMMER	AUTUMN	WINTER	height (cm)	spread (cm)	flower colour	
Leucojum aestivum	● ●		planting planting		60	20	☐	Flowers 2.5cm long
L. aestivum 'Gravetye Giant'	● ●		planting planting		75	25	☐	Flowers 4cm long
L. autumnale		planting	● ●		15	5	☐	Flowers 2cm long
L. nicaeense	● ●		planting planting		15	5	☐	Flowers 1.5cm long
L. vernum	●		planting planting	●	20	10	☐	Flowers 1.5cm long

 planting   flowering

Bulbs

L

Lilium
Lily
BULB

Lilies need very little introduction to gardeners. Their colourful summer flowers make them ideal choices for beds, borders and many are suitable for growing in containers. They also make perfect cut flowers for the home.

Lilium Citronella Group

Although numerous plants have lily in their common name, the true lilies are featured here. They vary in height, from dwarf species suitable for the front of the border and for growing in rock gardens, to tall types ideal for the back of mixed or herbaceous borders. The colour range is wide, thanks to extensive breeding in recent years. Many produce scented flowers that can, in some cases, be overpowering – some say even disagreeable!

There are several different types of true lilies, which are divided into a number of classifications.

Asiatic Hybrids (division I) have trumpet, bowl-shaped or turk's cap flowers up to 12.5cm (5in) across; bulbs should be spaced 45cm (18in) apart. The flowers can be upright (division Ia), outward-facing (division Ib) or pendent (division Ic).

Martagon Hybrids (division II) have turk's cap-shaped flowers up to 7.5cm (3in) across; spacing 30cm (12in).

Candidum Hybrids (division III) have trumpet-shaped flowers whose petals are strongly reflexed and up to 12.5cm (5in) across; spacing 30cm (12in).

American Hybrids (division IV) have flowers that are mainly turk's-cap shaped and up to 12.5cm (5in) across; spacing 45cm (18in).

Division V comprizes hybrids derived from *Lilium longiflorum* and *L. formosanum*. They are only half-hardy and not regularly offered.

Lilium Golden Splendor Group

Trumpet Hybrids can have trumpet (division VIa), bowl-shaped (division VIb), flat (division VIc) or recurved (division VId) flowers up to 20cm (8in) across; spacing 45cm (18in).

Oriental Hybrids (division VII) can also have trumpet-shaped (VIIa), bowl-shaped (VIIb), flat (VIIc) or recurved (VIId) flowers up to 30cm (12in) across; spacing 30–45cm

Lilium 'African Queen'

Lilium henryi

	SPRING	SUMMER	AUTUMN	WINTER	height (cm)	spread (cm)	flower colour	
Lilium African Queen Group	planting	● ●	planting planting		150	10	▨	Group VIa; stem-rooting
L. 'Apollo'	planting	● ● ●	planting planting		70	8	☐	Group Ia; stem-rooting
L. auratum	planting	● ● ●	planting ● planting		150	10	☐	Flowers white with gold band. Group IX; stem-rooting
L. 'Black Dragon'	planting	● ●	planting planting		150	10	▦	Group VIa; stem-rooting
L. candidum		● ●	planting planting		180	12	☐	Group IX; basal-rooting
L. 'Casa Blanca'	planting	● ● ●	planting planting		120	10	☐	Group VIIb; stem-rooting
L. Citronella Group	planting	●	planting planting		150	12	▨	Group Ic; stem-rooting
L. 'Connecticut King'	planting	● ●	planting planting		90	8	▨	Group Ia; stem-rooting
L. 'Enchantment'	planting	●	planting planting		90	8	▨	Group Ia; stem-rooting

Bulbs

🌱 *planting*   ● *flowering*

(12–18in) depending on height. **Division VIII** includes all other hybrids not in the other divisions, and **division IX** includes all species and their varieties and forms.

The bulbs are made up of soft, fleshy scales that are easily damaged and can dry out if left out of the ground for too long, so always handle carefully and plant immediately you get them home or they are delivered. The depth of planting depends on the type as they can either be stem rooting or basal rooting; the former produce roots above the bulb as well as below, so need deeper planting; details are given in the tables.

Some lily species – such as L. candidum, L. henryi, L. longiflorum, L. martagon, L. pardalinum and L. regale – are lime

Lilium martagon var. *album*

soil	Well-drained, moisture retentive soil, so add compost and coarse sand, at planting time	
site	Prefers some sun and light shade for part of the day. Give shade to the base of the plants	
planting	Stem-rooting lilies 15–20cm (6–8in) deep, basal-rooting types 5–7.5cm (2–3in) deep	
general care	Mulch after planting, in autumn and again in spring. Feed with a slow release fertilizer in spring and liquid feeds while growing	
pests & disease	Aphids, slugs, scarlet lily beetles, grey mould, basal rot and lily leaf blight are problems, as are viruses spread by aphids	

Lilium 'Journey's End'

Bulbs

	SPRING	SUMMER	AUTUMN	WINTER	height (cm)	spread (cm)	flower colour	
L. 'Fata Morgana'	planting	flowering	planting		90	8		Group Ia. Double flowers; stem-rooting
L. 'Garden Party'	planting	flowering	planting		50	5		Flowers white with yellow band. Group VII; stem-rooting
L. Golden Splendor Group	planting	flowering	planting		180	12		Flowers have burgundy bands. Group VIa; stem-rooting
L. 'Gran Cru'	planting	flowering	planting		90	8		Group Ia; stem-rooting
L. henryi	planting	flowering	planting/flowering		180	12		Group IX; stem-rooting
L. 'Journey's End'	planting	flowering	planting		160	12		Group VIId; stem-rooting
L. 'Joy'	planting	flowering	planting		75	8		Group VIIb; stem-rooting
L. 'King Pete'	planting	flowering	planting		90	8		Cream with orange marks. Group Ib; stem-rooting
L. lancifolium	planting	flowering	planting/flowering		125	10		Flowers have dark purple spots. Group IX; stem-rooting
L. lancifolium var. splendens	planting	flowering	planting		125	10		Flowers have black spots. Group IX; stem-rooting

  planting   flowering

loving or lime tolerant, but most need a lime-free soil. Modern hybrids will usually tolerate alkaline soils. As the bulbs like cool conditions it pays to shade the base of the stems, by growing low-growing plants in front of them, for example.

Although most lilies produce stout stems that can tolerate windy conditions, it pays to stake those growing taller than 90cm (3ft) wherever wind is a problem.

As flowers fade, remove them to prevent plants wasting energy on seed production. After flowering has finished keep the plants growing strongly – a weekly liquid feed is beneficial – so that they have plenty of energy to build up the bulbs for flowering the following year. Do not remove the stems until they die in autumn, then cut down to ground level. Nearly all types are perfectly hardy and can remain in the ground throughout winter, although a protective mulch can be beneficial in cold regions. After several years it pays to lift and divide them, and separate out the young bulbils.

If you want to use lilies for indoor decoration, it pays to remove the pollen-bearing anthers first to prevent them shedding pollen, which can stain materials.

Most lilies can be grown in containers – but especially the Asiatic, Oriental and Trumpet hybrids. Space the bulbs evenly, with at least 2.5cm (1in) between them and 13mm (0.5in) from the edge of the pot, and use a loam-based compost. The bulbs can remain in the containers for several years before they need removing and replanting.

Plants can be propagated by dividing mature clumps in autumn or spring, or by scaling. Some species produce bulbils in the leaf axils (see pp18–20 for further propagation details).

Lilium regale var. album

	SPRING	SUMMER	AUTUMN	WINTER	height (cm)	spread (cm)	flower colour
L. longiflorum		● ●			100	8	Group IX; stem-rooting
L. longiflorum 'White American'		● ●			100	10	Group IX; stem-rooting
L. martagon		● ●			180	15	Group IX; stem-rooting
L. martagon var. album		● ●			180	15	Group IX; stem-rooting
L. pardalinum		●			180	15	Group IX; basal-rooting
L. Pink Perfection Group		●			180	15	Group VIa; stem-rooting
L. pumilum		●			45	5	Group IX; stem-rooting
L. regale		● ●			150	10	Group IX; stem-rooting
L. 'Shuksan'		●			150	10	Group IV; basal-rooting
L. speciosum		●			150	10	Flowers have red markings. Group IX; stem-rooting
L. 'Star Gazer'		● ●			150	10	Group VIIc; stem-rooting
L. 'Sterling Star'		● ●			100	8	Group Ia; stem-rooting
L. x testaceum		● ●			125	8	Group IX; basal-rooting

planting   ● flowering

Muscari

Grape hyacinth
BULB

The muscaris get their common name from the attractive dense spikes of fragrant, globular flowers that resemble a bunch of grapes when in bud. They are easy to grow, undemanding plants that are often neglected in favour of more showy spring bulbs, which is a shame; they are versatile and bring a splash of colour to spring gardens.

Muscari azureum

soil	Will flourish and perform best if planted in well-drained soil
site	Grape hyacinths prefer to be in a position where there is good light
planting	Plant the bulbs 5–7.5cm (2–3in) deep and space them out 10cm (4in) apart
general care	Care and maintenance is fairly minimal. Allow the foliage to die down before removing it
pests & disease	Relatively trouble free. Pests and diseases do not usually cause any problems to this plant

Grape hyacinths associate well with other plants that flower at the same time, such as daffodils (Narcissus), tulips (Tulipa), hellebores (Helleborus), violas and primulas.

Being natives of the Mediterranean and South West Asia, they prefer a sunny position in a rockery or border. They will tolerate light shade, but deep shade often prevents flowering and produces tall, leggy plants. They can also be grown in front of shrubs and herbaceous plants in beds and borders, as well as naturalizing at the edge of light woodland – particularly *Muscari armeniacum* – and in grass.

Plants are easily grown in pots and containers outside or can be forced for blooming indoors from mid-winter to early spring. The flowering stems can be cut to add to small, indoor floral arrangements.

Most species seed themselves quite easily and where this could become a nuisance it pays to remove the flowerheads after flowering. *M. botryoides* is not so prolific, so makes a good choice where more restraint growth is needed.

Lift and divide bulbs every three to four years in summer when dormant and remove offsets after flowering to propagate.

Muscari armeniacum

	SPRING	SUMMER	AUTUMN	WINTER	height (cm)	spread (cm)	flower colour	
Muscari armeniacum	●		✂ ✂		20	5	▦	Flowers have a white rim and light fragrance
M. aucheri	● ●		✂ ✂		15	5	▦	Flowers have a white rim
M. azureum	●		✂ ✂		15	5	▦	Flowers have a darker stripe
M. botryoides	● ●		✂ ✂		15	5	▦	Flowers have a white rim
M. botryoides 'Album'	● ●		✂ ✂		15	5	☐	Slender spikes of fragrant flowers
M. comosum 'Plumosum'		● ●	✂ ✂		30	10	▦	Large, feathery flowers

 planting   flowering

Narcissus
Daffodil
Bulb

There are few more cheery spring sights than a mass of yellow daffodils showing their flowerheads off, even on the coldest of days. The range of cultivars and species is enormous, making the daffodils indispensable and highly versatile plants. Most flower in spring, although a few of the earlier ones will start flowering in late winter. The flower colours range from white to shades of yellow and orange-red or pink, as well as bicolours. There are singles as well as double-flowered forms.

Narcissus canaliculatus

There are choices for the rock garden, producing informal swathes in grass and on banks, in formal beds and borders – tall ones up to 60cm (24in) for the middle of borders, dwarf forms reaching no more than 10cm (4in) for the front – as well as growing in containers including forcing for indoors.

To make classification of all the various species and cultivars easier, Narcissi are split into 13 divisions. The correct terminology for the flower parts are corona (commonly called trumpet or cup) and perianth (commonly called petals). In the variety table, the first colour refers to the perianth and the second to the corona where there are two colours.

Narcissus bulbocodium

Division 1 Trumpet daffodils. One flower per stem – the trumpet at least as long as the petals.

Division 2 Large-cupped daffodils. One flower per stem, cup more than one-third the length of the petals.

Division 3 Small-cupped daffodils.

soil	Will flourish and perform best if planted in well-drained soil
site	Narcissus grows well in a sunny position, but most will tolerate light shade
planting	Cover bulb with twice its height of soil/compost; 10–20cm (4–8in) apart depending on growing height
general care	Keep the foliage growing for as long as possible – water and give a feed if necessary
pests & disease	Narcissus fly and eelworms can attack the bulbs and fungal rots can be a problem in cold, wet soils

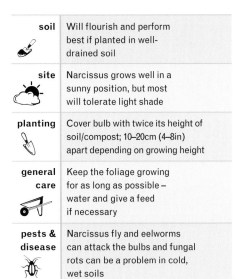

Narcissus 'Carlton'

Narcissus cyclamineus

One flower per stem, cup less than one-third the length of the petals.

Division 4 Double daffodils. One or more flowers per stem, with one or both of the flower parts doubled. Some in this group are derived from *Narcissus tazetta* and are scented.

Division 5 Triandrus daffodils. Usually two or more pendent flowers per stem, reflexed petals.

Narcissus 'Ice Follies'

Division 6 Cyclamineus daffodils. Usually one flower per stem, petals reflexed, flower at acute angle to the stem, short neck.

Division 7 Jonquilla and Apodanthus daffodils. Usually one to five flowers per stem, petals reflexed or spreading, flowers fragrant.

Division 8 Tazetta daffodils. Usually three to 20 flowers per stem, petals spreading not reflexed, flowers fragrant.

Division 9 Poeticus daffodils. Usually one flower per stem, petals white, cup usually

Narcissus 'Jack Snipe'

Narcissus 'February Gold'

	SPRING	SUMMER	AUTUMN	WINTER	height (cm)	spread (cm)	flower colour	
Narcissus 'Actaea'	●		🌱 🌱		40	15	▨	Division 9
N. 'Barrett Browning'	● ●		🌱 🌱		40	15	▨	Division 3
N. 'Birma'	●		🌱 🌱		40	15	▨	Division 3
N. bulbocodium	●		🌱 🌱		15	5	▢	Division 13
N. 'Bunting'	● ●		🌱 🌱		60	15	▨	Division 7
N. canaliculatus	● ●		🌱 🌱		15	5	▢	Division 13
N. 'Cantabile'	●		🌱 🌱		40	15	▨	Division 9
N. 'Carlton'	●		🌱 🌱		40	15	▢	Division 2
N. 'Cheerfulness'	●		🌱 🌱		40	15	▢	Division 4
N. cyclamineus	●		🌱 🌱	●	15	8	▢	Division 13

 planting ● flowering

disc-shaped with a green or yellow centre and red rim, flowers fragrant.

Division 10 Bulbocodium daffodils. Usually one flower per stem, petals insignificant compared to the prominent cup.

Division 11 Split-corona daffodils. Cup split rather than lobed and usually for more than half its length.

Division 12 Miscellaneous daffodils. All other daffodil cultivars not falling into one of the above categories

Division 13 Species daffodils.

Most of the daffodils in divisions 1, 2, 3, 4, 6, 9 and 12 are easy to grow and suitable for planting in mixed borders or naturalizing in grass. The triandrus hybrids (division 5) prefer warmer, very well-drained conditions and are better suited to warm positions at the front of borders or similar situations. The jonquils (division 7) also like a sunny, sheltered position but one which is not too dry. Some of the division 8 tazettas are not as hardy as others and are far better suited for growing indoors, or needing a warm, sheltered position in winter that gets baked in summer. *N.* 'Geranium', though, is an excellent choice for sunny borders.

The species, of which there are dozens but only a few of the most common are mentioned here, vary dramatically in their growing requirements. *N. bulbocodium*, the hoop petticoat, will grow in grass but is better on moist slopes or, failing that, a rock garden. *N. canaliculatus* needs a warm,

Narcissus 'Tahiti'

Narcissus 'Jenny'

Narcissus 'Little Beauty'

	SPRING	SUMMER	AUTUMN	WINTER	height (cm)	spread (cm)	flower colour	
N. 'February Gold'	●		🌱 🌱	●	30	8		Division 6
N. 'Geranium'	●		🌱 🌱		35	10		Division 8
N. 'Hawera'	●		🌱 🌱		20	8		Division 5
N. 'Ice Follies'	●		🌱 🌱		40	15		Division 2
N. 'Ice Wings'	●		🌱 🌱		25	10		Division 5
N. 'Jack Snipe'	● ●		🌱 🌱		20	8		Division 6
N. jonquilla	●		🌱 🌱		30	8		Division 13
N. 'Jumblie'	●		🌱 🌱		20	8		Division 12
N. 'Kenellis'	●		🌱 🌱		15	8		Division 10
N. 'Lemon Beauty'	●		🌱 🌱		25	10		Division 11
N. 'Little Beauty'	●		🌱 🌱		15	8		Division 1
N. 'Minnow'	● ●		🌱 🌱		15	8		Division 8
N. 'Mite'	●		🌱 🌱		23	10		Division 6
N. 'Mount Hood'	●		🌱 🌱		45	15		Division 1
N. obvallaris	●		🌱 🌱		25	8		Division 13

🌱 planting   ● flowering

Narcissus 'Mite'

sunny spot where the bulbs can ripen in summer. *N. cyclamineus* prefers moist soil and can even be grown at the edge of ponds or streams; most of its hybrids in division 6 prefer similar conditions. *N. jonquilla* is easy to grow providing you give it a sheltered, sunny position. *N. obvallaris*, the Tenby daffodil, is vigorous and ideal for growing in grass. *N. pseudonarcissus* is similar and an excellent choice for borders or growing in grass.

Narcissus pseudonarcissus

Daffodils are generally easy to look after and should be left in the ground to build up large clumps. To ensure regular flowering they should be fed with a low-nitrogen, high potash fertilizer; use a granular fertilizer in late winter and supplement with liquid feeds as the flowers fade and before the foliage dies down.

Plants can be propagated by lifting and removing offsets in autumn or lifting and dividing large, congested clumps as the leaves die down after flowering.

	SPRING	SUMMER	AUTUMN	WINTER	height (cm)	spread (cm)	flower colour	
N. 'Orangery'	● ●		🖐 🖐		35	10		Division 11
N. 'Passionale'	●		🖐 🖐		40	15		Division 2
N. 'Pipit'	●		🖐 🖐		15	8		Division 7. Cup fades to white
N. pseudonarcissus	●		🖐 🖐		20	10		Division 13
N. 'Quail'	● ●		🖐 🖐		25	10		Division 7
N. 'Rijnveld's Early Sensation'	●		🖐 🖐	●	25	10		Division 1
N. 'Rippling Waters'	● ●		🖐 🖐		40	15		Division 5
N. 'Rip Van Winkle'	●		🖐 🖐		15	8		Division 4
N. 'Saint Keverne'	● ●		🖐 🖐		40	15		Division 2
N. 'Sir Winston Churchill'	● ●		🖐 🖐		40	15		Division 4
N. 'Small Talk'	●		🖐 🖐		15	8		Division 1
N. 'Suzy'	●		🖐 🖐		40	8		Division 7
N. 'Tahiti'	●		🖐 🖐		40	15		Division 4
N. 'Tête-à-tête'	●		🖐 🖐	●	15	5		Division 12
N. 'Topolino'	●		🖐 🖐		25	10		Division 1

🖐 planting   ● flowering

Nectaroscordum

BULB

This stately, easy-to-grow plant with its multi-coloured flowers on tall stems is a perfect choice where a focal point in the garden is needed in spring. Nectaroscordums also look great when planted in beds and borders.

soil	Will flourish and perform best if planted in well-drained soil
site	Nectaroscordums grow best when planted in a sunny position
planting	Plant the bulbs 10cm (4in) deep and space them roughly 30cm (12in) apart
general care	Nectaroscordums are easy plants to look after, requiring very little if no attention at all
pests & disease	Onion white rot can be a problem, otherwise generally trouble free from most pests and diseases

The 2.5cm (1in) long, bell-shaped flowers hang down on thin stalks and are flushed pink and dark red with a greenish tinge. They are produced in loose clusters of up to 40 on top of tall stems. After flowering the stalks turn upwards to hold the seedpods erect. It seeds itself readily and can become invasive if allowed to do so, so unless seed is required it is a good idea to remove the seedheads. The dried stems and seedheads are much loved by flower arrangers and this is a good way of dealing with them to prevent seeding.

Both the flowers and the strap-like leaves have an onion smell and this plant used to be classified as an Allium – and is still sometimes offered as *Allium siculum*. The foliage emerges in spring but dies back quickly after flowering.

Nectaroscordums can also be naturalized in grassland – in fact, just about anywhere that does not dry out excessively in summer. When growing them in borders surround them with low-growing plants such as hostas, hellebores (Helleborus) and hardy geraniums (Geranium).

Overcrowded clumps can be split in autumn if flowering starts to decline.

Plants self propagate readily from seed or offsets can be removed in autumn.

Nectaroscordum siculum

	SPRING	SUMMER	AUTUMN	WINTER	height (cm)	spread (cm)	flower colour	
Nectaroscordum siculum	● ●		✂ ✂		100	30		Flowers shaded purple-red
N. siculum subsp. *bulgaricum*	● ●		✂ ✂		100	30		Flowers shaded pink and green, and larger than species

✂ planting   ● flowering

Nerine
BULB

Nerines with their long-lived almost spidery, star-shaped flowers add a bright splash of colour to the garden, greenhouse or conservatory in autumn at a time when other plants are past their best.

The flowerheads of the nerines consist of a cluster of funnel-shaped blooms with narrow, wavy petals that curl backwards. These appear at the top of graceful stems and last well in water when cut for indoors. The strap-shaped foliage usually appears after flowering and dies down in late spring or summer.

Only *Nerine bowdenii* is hardy enough to grow permanently outside – tolerating temperatures down to -15°C (5°F) – but even then needs the warmest conditions you can provide. It cannot take these temperatures in combination with winter wet, so some protection will be needed including covering with open-ended cloches and mulching with sharp

Nerine 'Zeal Giant'

sand or bark. The other option is to plant in containers of loam-based compost and bring them into the protection of a greenhouse or conservatory for winter.

N. sarniensis, the Guernsey lily, needs to be grown as a greenhouse or conservatory plant. Plant bulbs in late summer and begin watering when the flower buds appear. Keep the compost just moist through winter and maintain 10–13°C (50–55°F). When the foliage is fully developed, feed weekly with a liquid fertilizer for two months. Once foliage starts to turn yellow, stop watering and feeding.

The bulbs are best left undisturbed, but overcrowded bulbs can be lifted and divided in summer when the foliage has died down. Remove offsets when fully detached from the parent bulb.

Nerine bowdenii

soil	Plant in a loam-based compost for indoors or good, well-drained soil outside
site	Good light indoors, sheltered position in full sun outside – preferably base of a warm wall
planting	Plant with the neck of the bulb above the compost, or 10cm (4in) deep in soil; 15cm (6in) apart
general care	Little care and maintenance needed. Feed in early spring with a granular or controlled-release fertilizer
pests & disease	Slugs and snails can be problematic to nerines. Mealy bug may attack indoor plants.

	SPRING	SUMMER	AUTUMN	WINTER	height (cm)	spread (cm)	flower colour	
Nerine bowdenii	🌱🌱		● ●		60	15	▨	Flowerheads up to 15cm (6in) across
N. bowdenii 'Alba'	🌱🌱		● ●		60	15	▢	Flowers have a pink flush
N. bowdenii 'Pink Triumph'	🌱🌱		● ●		60	15	▦	Flowers have a silvery sheen
N. sarniensis		🌱	● ● ●		45	15	▨	Flowers may sometimes be red or white
N. 'Stephanie'	🌱🌱	🌱	● ●		45	15	▢	Can be grown outside
N. 'Zeal Giant'		🌱	● ●		60	15	▦	Large flowerheads

 planting   flowering

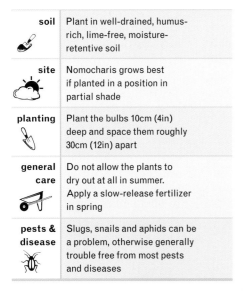

Nomocharis
BULB

This showy plant from the Himalayas and Western China is a perfect choice for cool, moist climates where the soil never dries out. Although growing these lily-like plants can be a bit of a challenge, it is a challenge worth accepting if you can provide the right conditions for good, healthy growth – an eye-catching display of flowers. They are perfect for woodland gardens. *Nomocharis saluenensis* is the easiest to grow.

soil	Plant in well-drained, humus-rich, lime-free, moisture-retentive soil
site	Nomocharis grows best if planted in a position in partial shade
planting	Plant the bulbs 10cm (4in) deep and space them roughly 30cm (12in) apart
general care	Do not allow the plants to dry out at all in summer. Apply a slow-release fertilizer in spring
pests & disease	Slugs, snails and aphids can be a problem, otherwise generally trouble free from most pests and diseases

The saucer-shaped or flattened star-shaped flowers up to 10cm (4in) across are produced in groups of up to 10 on each stem. The petals are attractively marked with deeper spots and central blotches and are often finely fringed. The lance-shaped, deep green leaves are up to 10cm (4in) long and are produced in whorls around the flower stem.

Nomocharis looks excellent when grown in association with blue Himalayan poppies (Meconopsis) and enjoys the same soil and aspect conditions. Top dress the soil in spring with leafmould or compost before growth begins to top up the soil's humus content.

Although dried bulbs are available it is usually better to choose pot-grown plants since the bulbs dislike being lifted and dried. If buying bulbs, get them as early as possible and plant immediately. Planting the bulbs first in pots and then planting out into the garden is often a better way to deal with them.

Plants dislike disturbance, so buy new bulbs or plants rather than trying to propagate them.

Nomocharis aperta

	SPRING	SUMMER	AUTUMN	WINTER	height (cm)	spread (cm)	flower colour	
Nomocharis aperta	planting	flowering		planting	60	15		Flowers have red spots and maroon base
N. pardanthina	planting	flowering		planting	90	15		Flowers have dark purple base
N. saluenensis	planting	flowering		planting	75	15		Flowers flushed deep pink at the tips

 planting   flowering

Bulbs

N

Notholirion

BULB

Notholirions are grown for their delicate, trumpet-shaped flowers in shades of lilacs and pinks which are carried on slender stems. The flowers are up to 4cm (1½in) long and produced at the top of the stems in groups of up to 20 in the case of *Notholirion bulbuliferum*, although *N. macrophyllum* only produces up to seven flowers per stem.

The long narrow leaves are produced in basal clumps and, in some species, can appear in winter or early spring. Even though the plants are hardy, the foliage tends to be damaged by heavy frosts. It is

soil	Will flourish if planted in well-drained, humus-rich soils
site	Prefers dappled or partial shade and will not tolerate full sun
planting	Plant the bulbs 10cm (4in) deep and space them roughly 30cm (12in) apart
general care	Notholirions are fairly easy plants to look after, requiring very little if no attention at all
pests & disease	Relatively trouble free. Pests and diseases do not usually cause any problems to this plant

Notholirion bulbuliferum

a good idea, therefore, to plant near low-growing evergreens so that these can afford some winter protection to Notholirion's foliage.

Another option is to grow the plants in pots in a cold greenhouse. Plant in a loam-based compost and grow in bright, filtered light. Water the compost regularly and thoroughly when plants are in growth, but withhold water when the bulbs are dormant, keeping the compost just sufficiently moist to prevent the bulbs drying out.

Like Cardiocrinum, this genus is unusual in that individual bulbs die after flowering; planting a few bulbs over three years will ensure you have plants in flower every year.

Plants are propagated by removing and replanting offsets in autumn which may take two or three years to reach flowering size.

	SPRING	SUMMER	AUTUMN	WINTER	height (cm)	spread (cm)	flower colour	
Notholirion bulbuliferum		● ●	⚘ ⚘		90	10		Petals have greenish tips
N. macrophyllum		● ●	⚘ ⚘		45	8		Flowers are purple-spotted, pale lavender within

 planting   flowering

Ornithogalum

Star of Bethlehem
or Chincherinchee
BULB

The ornithogalums are grown for their attractive star-shaped flowers that are usually white and which are particularly useful for brightening up shady areas of the garden.

Ornithogalum umbellatum

Ornithogalum nutans

There are two distinct types of ornithogalums – those that are hardy and can be grown outside, and those which cannot tolerate frosts and are either grown as indoor pot plants or planted outside in spring and lifted in autumn.

Chincherinchee, *Ornithogalum thyrsoides*, is the best known of the non-hardy species. It produces dense, conical spikes of cup-shaped flowers 2.5cm (1in) wide that are white with green stripes on the reverse.

The bulbs can be planted in pots in autumn for planting outside in late spring, or planted directly in the ground in spring. Either planting time can be used for growing the plants permanently in pots in a cool greenhouse or conservatory. Plant six bulbs per 15cm (6in) pot, keep the compost moist but

soil	For best results, plant in any well-drained soil or potting compost
site	Ornithogalums grow well if positioned in either full sun or partial shade
planting	Plant outdoors 7.5cm (3in) deep and 7.5-10cm (3-4in) apart; plant *O. thyrsoides* 5cm (2in) deep
general care	Generally, care and maintenance for these plants is straightforward. Deadhead plants after the flowers fade
pests & disease	Relatively trouble free. Pests and diseases do not usually cause any problems to this plant

reduce watering once flowering is over and repot when needed. They need a minimum winter temperature of 7°C (45°F). The cut flowers can last for several weeks in a cool room if the stems are cut when in bud.

The hardy species look best when planted in informal groups and will grow in short grass, at the front of beds and borders or on rock gardens. Once they become established they soon put on good displays. *O. umbellatum* and to a lesser extent *O. nutans* soon become large plants only suited to larger rockeries and may need lifting and dividing to prevent them becoming a nuisance.

Plants are propagated by lifting and dividing clumps when they are dormant; autumn for spring-flowering types and spring for summer-flowering types.

	SPRING	SUMMER	AUTUMN	WINTER	height (cm)	spread (cm)	flower colour
Ornithogalum dubium	●		🪏 🪏	● ● ●	30	10	Red, yellow or white-flowered forms available
O. narbonense	● ●		🪏 🪏		90	15	Flowers borne in pyramidal clusters
O. nutans	● ●		🪏 🪏		45	10	Flowers have a green midrib
O. thyrsoides	🪏 🪏	● ● ●	🪏		40	10	Flowers are good for cutting and last well
O. umbellatum	● ●		🪏 🪏		30	10	Can become invasive

🪏 *planting*   *flowering*

Oxalis

BULB, TUBER *or* RHIZOME

Oxalis have plenty going for them as garden and indoor plants. A long flowering period and attractive foliage that can in some species be used for ground cover add up to an all-round winner.

The flat or cup-shaped flowers are up to 3cm (1¼in) wide and produced over the summer months. They are beautifully set off by the clover-like compound leaves, made up of three or more leaflets, which are usually attractive in their own right. Both the flowers and leaves may close up at night or when the sun goes in during the day.

The species vary in their hardiness, some being frost hardy while others need to be grown inside. The hardy oxalis species, *Oxalis adenophylla* and *O. enneaphylla*, are best suited to a sunny position on a rock garden, edging the front of beds and borders, growing through gravel in paths or in pots on sunny patios. However, they will appreciate shading from hot summer sunlight.

O. versicolor is not hardy and should be grown in pots in a cool greenhouse or conservatory at a minimum temperature of

soil	These plants are relatively unfussy, as long as the soil is well-drained
site	Oxalis are best suited to a sunny position in the garden
planting	Plant 7.5cm (3in) deep and space them roughly 10cm (4in) apart
general care	Care and maintenance for these plants is straightforward. Lift and divide congested clumps of plants
pests & disease	Usually trouble free from pests and diseases, however, slugs can cause problems to this plant

16°C (60°F). It needs plenty of water, regular liquid feeds when in full growth, high humidity and shading from strong sunlight.

O. tetraphylla and *O. triangularis* are moderately hardy and may tolerate a few degrees of short-term frost and should be planted where the roots are protected from frosts. To be on the safe side, they can be grown in a cold greenhouse or conservatory at a minimum temperature of 7°C (45°F).

The oxalis are a mixed group concerning their rootstocks. *O. tetraphylla* and *O. versicolor* grow from bulbs; *O. enneaphylla* and *O. triangularis* produce rhizomes; and *O. adenophylla* produces tubers. Those grown from bulbs can be propagated from offsets after flowering. Those producing tubers and rhizomes can be divided in spring.

Oxalis triangularis

	SPRING	SUMMER	AUTUMN	WINTER	height (cm)	spread (cm)	flower colour
Oxalis adenophylla					10	15	Grey-blue foliage
O. enneaphylla					8	15	Grey-blue foliage
O. tetraphylla					15	15	Large leaves of four triangular leaflets with purple bases
O. triangularis					15	15	Reddish-purple foliage
O. triangularis subsp. *papilionacea*					15	15	Green foliage
O. versicolor					10	25	Flowers have crimson margins below

🌱 *planting*   ✺ *flowering*

Paradisea

Paradise lily *or*
St Bruno's lily

RHIZOME

The tall spikes of white, almost translucent, sweet smelling flowers make paradise lilies a must for any garden, where they will brighten up even the dullest of shady corners.

There are only two species in this genus. *Paradisea liliastrum* is the shorter and has the least but largest (5cm/2in long) flowers per stem, whereas *P. lusitanica* is taller and tougher with more 4cm (1½in) long flowers per stem. The petal-like tepals of

Paradisea liliastrum

P. liliastrum have a green spot at the tip. The broad, grass-like, grey-green foliage helps to offset the flowers and is ornamental in its own right.

Paradiseas are perfect for growing in herbaceous and mixed borders as well as lightly shaded rock gardens and naturalizing in grass, and *P. lusitanica*,

soil	Needs a well-drained, humus-rich soil that does not dry out in summer
site	Paradisea grows well in both light shade or a partially sunny position
planting	Plant the rhizomes 7.5cm (3in) deep and space them 30cm (12in) apart
general care	Generally, top dress established clumps with compost or well-rotted manure in autumn
pests & disease	Usually trouble free from pests and diseases, but slugs and snails may cause a few problems

which forms dense spreading clumps, is useful for colonizing banks and growing at the edge of woodland or around shrubs.

The rhizomes produce fleshy roots and are generally not offered for sale as dormant roots – pot-grown plants being the most common planting material. Where dormant roots are available buy them early in the year and plant as soon as possible.

Plants can be propagated by lifting and dividing the rhizomes in spring or after flowering. However, carry this out only when really necessary because the plants dislike disturbance and only a few flowers may appear in the year following the transplanting.

Snails and, particularly, slugs can take a real fancy to Paradisea, so try and protect plants by following one of the methods outlined in the Pests and Diseases section on pages 140–1.

Paradisea liliastrum

	SPRING	SUMMER	AUTUMN	WINTER	height (cm)	spread (cm)	flower colour	
Paradisea liliastrum	🌱	● ●			60	45	☐	Stems bear 3 to 10 funnel-shaped flowers
P. lusitanica	🌱	●			75	45	☐	Stems bear 20–25 bell-shaped flowers

🌱 planting   ● flowering

P

Bulbs

Polianthes
Tuberose
TUBER

The tuberose was a firm favourite of people in the mid- to late 19th century, being grown in conservatories for its waxy white highly fragrant – almost overpowering – flowers. It is becoming increasingly popular once more.

The 2.5cm (1in) long flowers are produced on the top half of the tall stems, the petals opening out to produce a star. Each tuber produces from two to six stems. The cultivar 'The Pearl' is more common than the species and has shorter flower spikes of double flowers that are just as fragrant.

Polianthes tuberosa

Polianthes are normally grown as greenhouse or conservatory plants. Pot up the tubers in moist compost in spring at a temperature of 15–18°C (60–65°F) and do not water the compost until the leaves appear. Then water freely and feed fortnightly with a liquid fertilizer when in growth. When the flowers are just beginning to open the stems can be cut for indoor arrangements, or the pots stood outside on a warm patio for the summer, or placed in a conservatory or in the house.

Successional plantings in autumn and spring can produce plants that will provide flowers for many months; maintain a minimum temperature of 15°C (60°F).

When the flowers are over and the leaves start to die down stop watering. Although it is normally recommended to dispose of the tubers once they have flowered, drying them off for the winter and storing them in frost-free conditions may keep them going from year to year.

In very warm areas it may even be possible to grow the plants outside at the foot of a warm, sunny, sheltered wall from a mid-spring planting. Lift the tubers once the foliage dies back and store in nearly dry sand in a cool, frost-free place.

Plants can be propagated by removing offsets at planting time, but they may not be ripe enough to flower.

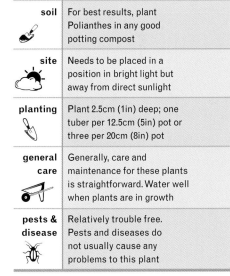

soil	For best results, plant Polianthes in any good potting compost
site	Needs to be placed in a position in bright light but away from direct sunlight
planting	Plant 2.5cm (1in) deep; one tuber per 12.5cm (5in) pot or three per 20cm (8in) pot
general care	Generally, care and maintenance for these plants is straightforward. Water well when plants are in growth
pests & disease	Relatively trouble free. Pests and diseases do not usually cause any problems to this plant

P

Bulbs

	SPRING	SUMMER	AUTUMN	WINTER	height (cm)	spread (cm)	flower colour	
Polianthes tuberosa	planting planting	flowering flowering flowering	flowering planting planting		100	40		Flowers are up to 5cm (2in) long
P. tuberosa 'The Pearl'	planting planting	flowering flowering flowering	flowering planting planting		60	25		Double flowers

 planting ● flowering

Puschkinia
Striped squill
BULB

This single species genus closely related to Scilla and Chionodoxa is tough, hardy and trouble free, and produces dense spikes of very attractive spring flowers. The 10cm (4in) long flower spikes carry between six and 12 open, bell-shaped flowers, 1cm (½in), long among the dark green, strap-like leaves.

Puschkinia scilloides var. libanotica

Puschkinia scilloides

The best place for puschkinias is in the rock garden or other well-drained area. In heavy soils it pays to add sharp sand or grit to the soil at planting time to help improve drainage. They make excellent border edging plants and can be naturalized in short grass. You can even grow them around trees and shrubs, but make sure they get a good amount of sunlight.

They also grow well in pots and other containers – both outdoors and in; growing them in pots allows you to appreciate the flowers close up. For growing in a cool greenhouse plant seven or eight bulbs in a 15cm (6in) half pot or pan of loam-based compost. Plunge the pots outside for six to eight weeks and bring inside from mid-winter onwards. When in growth keep the compost moist at all times, but after flowering gradually reduce the watering. Repot the following autumn.

Flowering is always best in positions where the bulbs can dry out in summer and so growing them close to plants that need watering in summer is not a good idea.

They look best when planted in large clumps although the bulbs will increase quickly to make good-sized clumps in only a few years.

Plants are propagated by removing offsets from dormant bulbs in late summer and replanting immediately.

soil	For best results, plant Puschkinia in any well-drained soil
site	These plants grow well if positioned in either full sun or light shade
planting	Plant the bulbs 5cm (2in) deep and space them roughly 7.5cm (3in) apart
general care	Apply a slow-release fertilizer when the foliage starts to emerge. Remove faded foliage once it has completely died back
pests & disease	Relatively trouble free. Pests and diseases do not usually cause any problems to this plant

	SPRING	SUMMER	AUTUMN	WINTER	height (cm)	spread (cm)	flower colour	
Puschkinia scilloides	● ●		✎ ✎		15	8		Flowers have a dark blue stripe
P. scilloides var. *libanotica*	● ●		✎ ✎		15	8		Produces smaller flowers

✎ planting   ● flowering

Ranunculus

Persian
buttercup

<small>TUBEROUS ROOT</small>

The buttercups contain numerous species, some of which are weeds. There are a couple of species that produce perennial roots that could be included here, but only cultivars of *Ranunculus asiaticus* are commonly grown.

The Persian buttercup produces flowers that are up to 10cm (4in) across in a range of colours from white through yellow and orange to pink and red. There are a number of flower forms available including singles, semi-doubles and doubles. The Persian group often produce single flowers, the French group are semi-double, paeony-flowered are large and often fully double and the most popular Turban group are fully double and often ball like. The flowers are excellent for cutting as they last well in water.

The attractive, deeply cut, almost ferny foliage appears in spring and dies down in summer after flowering is over.

Persian buttercups can be bought as tubers and planted in spring or autumn (mild areas only), or as potted plants in spring. It is usually sold as a mixture of colours and, as a result, plants are best bought when they are just coming into bud so you can see the intended flower colour. Plants will flower in

soil	For best results, plant Ranunculus in any well-drained soil
site	These plants require a sheltered position preferably in full sun
planting	Plant the tuberous roots 2.5cm (1in) deep and space them 15cm (6in) apart
general care	In general, feed with a granular fertilizer in spring and water plants in prolonged dry weather
pests & disease	Aphids may be a problem, as can mildew in dry weather, but otherwise fairly trouble free from pests and diseases

late spring and early summer, those set out in spring will flower in early and mid-summer.

The tubers should be soaked in tepid water for a few hours before planting with the 'claws' facing down. They are not completely hardy and, although they can be left in the ground over winter in mild areas, are best lifted when the leaves turn yellow, dried in the sun and stored in dry compost in a cool, but frost-free airy place.

Plants are propagated by separating the tubers at lifting time.

R

Bulbs

Ranunculus Bloomingdale Series

	SPRING	SUMMER	AUTUMN	WINTER	height (cm)	spread (cm)	flower colour	
Ranunculus Bloomingdale Series	🖐 🖐 ●	● ● ●	🖐 🖐		30	15		Double flowers
R. French group	🖐 🖐 ●	● ● ●	🖐 🖐		30	15		Semi-double flowers
R. peony-flowered	🖐 🖐 ●	● ● ●	🖐 🖐		30	15		Semi-double flowers
R. Tecolote Hybrids	🖐 🖐 ●	● ● ●	🖐 🖐		35	15		Large double flowers

 planting   flowering

Rhodohypoxis
Red star
CORM

Rhodohypoxis are invaluable garden and cool greenhouse plants for one very good reason – they make low carpets covered in charming flowers that are produced for months on end.

The corm-like rootstocks produce tufts of hairy, pale or dull green leaves that are around 5cm (2in) long and the 1.5–2cm (½–¾in) wide flowers rise above these.

Being a native of South Africa plants are not reliably hardy; although they will tolerate temperatures down to -5°C (34°F) or more, they hate winter wet demanding dry conditions when they are dormant. This can be achieved by covering the plants with open-ended cloches. Because of their size and site and soil requirements, red stars are best grown in sunny rock gardens.

If you can provide suitable winter conditions then plants can be left outside all year round, otherwise grow them in containers that can be brought into a frost-free greenhouse for the winter or grow them permanently in the greenhouse where their flowers can be appreciated close up. Water plants regularly when in growth but stop watering as the plants die back and keep the compost almost dry during the winter. Start plants back into growth in early spring.

Rhodohypoxis 'Fred Broome'

Although it is possible to buy the corm-like rootstocks you are more likely to find pot-grown plants in the alpine sections of nurseries and garden centres. Numerous named cultivars are now available.

Plants are propagated by dividing the clustered corms in late spring. It is a good idea to do this every three to four years to keep plants healthy and flowering freely.

Rhodohypoxis baurii

Rhodohypoxis 'Albrighton'

soil	Needs a well-drained, gritty, humus-rich soil that is lime free and does not dry out in summer
site	These plants need full sun, but prefer light shade in extremely hot areas
planting	Plant corms 2.5–5cm (1–2in) deep and space them roughly 10–15cm (4–6in) apart
general care	Protect from excessive winter wet and spring frosts. Water carefully during hot, dry weather, avoiding wetting the foliage
pests & disease	Mice may eat the corms, but otherwise pests and diseases do not usually cause any problems to this plant

	SPRING	SUMMER	AUTUMN	WINTER	height (cm)	spread (cm)	flower colour	
Rhodohypoxis 'Albrighton'					10	5		Smaller flowers
R. baurii					10	5		Flowers borne on hairy stems
R. 'Fred Broome'					10	5		Flowers have firm, broad petals
R. 'Ruth'					10	5		Large flowers

🛠 planting   ✺ flowering

R

Bulbs

Roscoea
TUBEROUS ROOT

These plants produce gorgeous, handsome and somewhat unusual orchid-like tubular flowers over several weeks. Despite their exotic look roscoeas are not especially difficult to grow.

soil	Roscoea prefers any well-drained, humus-rich, preferably lime free, soil
site	These plants grow best in full sun but will tolerate light shade
planting	Plant the tuberous roots 15cm (6in) deep and space them roughly 15cm (6in) apart
general care	Generally, care and maintenance for these plants is straightforward. Deadhead plants after the flowers fade
pests & disease	Slugs, snails, wireworm and vine weevil may be a problem. Fungal diseases can be a problem in damp soils

The attractive flowers are borne in succession on short stems over a long time, usually one at a time, although *Roscoea cautleyoides* produces four or so flowers at a time. The usually lance-shaped leaves are between 20–35cm (8–14in) long depending on the species. The plants die down in autumn, rest for a long time and emerge again in the warmth of late spring.

This is a plant for the rock garden, front of a border or woodland garden where it will receive plenty of sunlight.

Plants will benefit from regular watering during long periods of drought. Roscoeas are hardy down to -20°C (-4°F), providing they are planted at the correct depth in well-drained soil and covered with a thick protective mulch of bark, compost or leafmould.

The tuberous roots can be divided and replanted in spring or as soon as the foliage dies down, although they dislike too much disturbance. The species, especially *R. cautleyoides*, can readily self seed after a good summer.

R

Bulbs

Roscoea 'Beesiana'

	SPRING	SUMMER	AUTUMN	WINTER	height (cm)	spread (cm)	flower colour
Roscoea auriculata	🛠	● ● ●	🛠 🛠		55	25	Flowers 5cm long
R. 'Beesiana'	🛠	● ● ●	🛠 🛠		45	20	The 5cm flowers are sometimes streaked with purple
R. cautleyoides	🛠	● ●	🛠 🛠		50	15	Flowers 4cm long
R. purpurea	🛠	● ● ●	🛠 ● 🛠		30	20	The 6cm flowers may be purple and white or all white

 planting   flowering

Scadoxus

Blood flower
BULB

Scadoxus, which resemble the closely-related Haemanthus and are sometimes still listed as Haemanthus, are grown for their spectacular flowers with prominent stamens that give rise to the common name.

Scadoxus differ from Haemanthus in that the flowerheads are ball-shaped and much larger, comprising up to 200 individual flowers, and there are no bracts at the base. The broad, lanced-shaped basal leaves are arranged in a basal rosette.

possible. Because they hate root disturbance they can stay in the same pot for several years. Only repot when absolutely necessary as growth restarts in spring.

Plants need a minimum temperature of 10–15°C (50–60°F) and grown in bright but diffused light. Move Scadoxus into part shade when the flower buds begin to colour to preserve the colour and prolong the flowering period. Those grown as houseplants can tolerate lower temperatures providing they are grown in good light. They prefer a humid atmosphere around the leaves so mist regularly or stand pots on saucers of damp grit.

Keep the compost slightly damp when the bulbs are dormant in winter, but water well when in growth.

Plants can be propagated by removing offsets when growth begins in spring. Carefully remove them, pot up and keep in a covered propagator or similar.

Scadoxus multiflorus

Scadoxus are perfect for cool greenhouses and conservatories, but they can be moved outside to a warm, sheltered patio in summer. They prefer to be under-potted, so always use as small a pot as

soil	Pot up using a loam-based compost with added grit in a pot twice the diameter of the bulb
site	Grow Scadoxus in a brightly lit position, but keep out of strong, direct sunlight
planting	Plant with the tip just above the surface of the compost; one bulb per pot
general care	Water and feed with a liquid fertilizer regularly when in growth, but keep the compost just damp at other times
pests & disease	Mealy bug may be a problem, but otherwise pests and diseases do not usually trouble this plant

	SPRING	SUMMER	AUTUMN	WINTER	height (cm)	spread (cm)	flower colour	
Scadoxus multiflorus	🛠 🛠	✺ ✺			75	45	▨	Flowerheads up to 15cm across
S. multiflorus subsp. *katherinae*	🛠 🛠	✺ ✺			100	45	▨	Flowerheads up to 20cm across

🛠 planting   ✺ flowering

Schizostylis

Kaffir lily

RHIZOME

The kaffir lily will bring a bright splash of colour to beds and borders from late summer through the autumn. The star-shaped flowers measure up to 4cm (1½in) across and are produced in groups of up to ten on slender stems. Flower colour can be white or shades of pink or red depending on cultivar. They make good cut flowers for indoor decoration. The flowers appear above the narrow, sword-shaped, ribbed foliage.

Native to the damp meadows of southern Africa, Schizostylis need a moisture retentive soil, so add plenty of humus at planting time. Mulching the soil in late spring will also help retain soil moisture. They can even be grown in moist soil beside a pool or stream, providing it does not remain waterlogged for more than a month or so.

It pays to remove the flowers as they fade and remove dead foliage in late autumn. The plants may be short lived in cold areas, so protect the crowns with a thick mulch of composted bark or leafmould in the autumn once the foliage has been removed.

Plants are hardy to between -5 and -10°C (14–23°F) and can be grown in pots in a cool greenhouse, especially in areas where autumn temperatures drop suddenly.

Under favourable conditions plants soon become congested and you should lift and divide overcrowded clumps every

Schizostylis coccinea 'Jennifer'

three to four years in spring. Plants can be propagated by dividing the rhizomes at the same time.

Schizostylis coccinea 'Major'

soil	For best results, plant in any good, moisture retentive soil
site	Schizostylis prefers to be sited in a warm, sunny position
planting	Plant the rhizomes 5cm (2in) deep and space them about 25–30cm (10–12in) apart
general care	Water plants regularly during prolonged periods of dry weather, as the fleshy roots are prone to drying out
pests & disease	Usually trouble free from most pests and diseases, but slugs may damage young shoots

	SPRING	SUMMER	AUTUMN	WINTER	height (cm)	spread (cm)	flower colour	
Schizostylis coccinea	🌱🌱🌱		● ● ●		60	30	▨	Flower spikes up to 23cm long
S. coccinea f. alba	🌱🌱🌱		● ● ●		45	25	☐	Shorter lived and less hardy
S. coccinea 'Jennifer'	🌱🌱🌱		● ●		60	30	▨	Larger flowers
S. coccinea 'Major'	🌱🌱🌱		● ● ●		60	30	▨	Larger flowers
S. coccinea 'Mrs Hegarty'	🌱🌱🌱		● ●		60	30	▨	Later flowering
S. coccinea 'Sunrise'	🌱🌱🌱		● ●		60	30	☐	Larger flowers

 planting   *flowering*

Scilla
Squill
BULB

The scillas are among the most dainty and attractive low-growing bulbs which, depending on the species chosen, will produce their starry or bell-shaped flowers in late winter, spring or early summer.

Scilla siberica

The flowers, in shades of blue and purple, although several species have a white-flowered form, are held on leafless stems among the mid-green, strap-shaped leaves.

Nearly all the species listed perform well on rock gardens and raised beds. *Scilla bifolia* and *S. siberica* can be naturalized in short grass or wild gardens. *S. bifolia* is also good for underplanting shrubs where it will benefit from the light shade. *S. mischtschenkoana* needs even better drainage than the others. All can be grown in containers and are especially useful for cold greenhouses. The winter- and spring-flowering species can also be grown indoors where they will flower a month or so earlier than normal.

The bluebells (now called Hyacinthoides) are sometimes still listed as scillas.

Although most scillas are hardy down to -15°C (5°F), *S. peruviana* will only tolerate temperatures down to -5°C (23°F) and should be mulched in late autumn with compost or leafmould to protect against cold weather. All scillas will benefit from mulching to help top up soil humus levels.

Once established they are best left

Scilla mischtschenkoana

Scilla peruviana

soil	This plant needs a well-drained, humus-rich, moisture-retentive soil
site	Grows well in sun or partial or dappled shade. *S. peruviana* needs a dry, sunny position
planting	Plant the bulbs 5–7.5cm (2–3in) deep and space them 5–7.5cm (2–3in) apart
general care	Scillas require very little in the way of care and attention – the plants generally take care of themselves
pests & disease	Relatively trouble free from pests and diseases, but mould can affect stored bulbs

undisturbed as long as they are growing and flowering well.

Plants can be propagated by lifting and removing offsets in late summer, but these are not produced freely – only every five years or so.

	SPRING	SUMMER	AUTUMN	WINTER	height (cm)	spread (cm)	flower colour	
Scilla bifolia	●	⚒ ⚒		●	15	8		Starry, fragrant flowers
S. mischtschenkoana	●	⚒ ⚒		●	15	5		Flowers have deep blue stripe
S. peruviana	● ●	⚒ ⚒			30	15		Dense flowerheads of starry flowers
S. siberica	● ●	⚒ ⚒			15	8		Bell-shaped flowers
S. siberica 'Spring Beauty'	● ●	⚒ ⚒			20	10		Vigorous plants

⚒ planting   ● flowering

Sisyrinchium
TUBER

Sisyrinchiums are invaluable garden plants, producing attractive clumps of narrow, sword-like evergreen foliage that forms handsome fans, and they flower throughout summer.

The plants produce spikes of starry flowers, as in *Sisyrinchium californicum*, or cup-shaped flowers, as in *S. striatum*, around 1cm (⅜in) wide. Individually, the flowers are not long lived, but are produced in succession over several weeks.

The taller types are best suited to growing in well-drained beds and borders, the shorter ones for rock gardens. Some species are tender and need to be grown in a cool greenhouse, but all those mentioned here are hardy down to between -10°C and -15°C (5–14°F).

Although the plants like plenty of moisture, they also need good drainage otherwise the foliage tends to become blackened and unsightly in soils that are wet over winter. Improve drainage by adding plenty of humus and even sharp sand at planting time. Some of the larger perennials, such as *S. californicum*, are shallow rooted and prone to die suddenly after several years.

S. californicum produces yellow flowers on stems up to 45cm (18in) high. The shorter *S. californicum* Brachypus Group is perhaps a better choice to grow and is very well suited to rockeries.

Although some suppliers provide dormant tubers, sisyrinchiums are usually bought as growing plants that are best planted in spring.

Plants are propagated by dividing mature clumps in spring. Plants readily self seed and the seedlings can become a nuisance if left. Unless seeds and seedlings are needed, it pays to remove the faded flowerheads.

Sisyrinchium striatum

soil	This plant needs a well-drained, humus-rich soil for it to thrive
site	Sisyrinchium requires a position in full sun for best results
planting	Plant tubers 5cm (2in) deep and space them roughly 10–30cm (4–12in) apart
general care	Keep young plants well watered until established. Remove discoloured foliage and faded flowerheads as they appear
pests & disease	Usually trouble free, however fungal disease can be problematic in damp soils

S

Bulbs

	SPRING	SUMMER	AUTUMN	WINTER	height (cm)	spread (cm)	flower colour	
Sisyrinchium californicum Brachypus Group					15	15		Grey-green foliage
S. macrocarpon					20	8		Flowers have a dark red ring in the centre
S. striatum					60	30		Flowers have purplish veins on the back
S. striatum 'Aunt May'					45	30		Foliage striped with cream and grey-green

 planting   flowering

Sparaxis

Harlequin flower
CORM

The half-hardy South African Sparaxis produces lots of attractive, starry flowers and is best grown in a cold or cool greenhouse or conservatory where the brilliant blooms will provide a riot of colour. The wiry stems produce loose heads of up to five starry flowers up to 5cm (2in) across above narrow, sword-shaped leaves.

The species listed, especially *Sparaxis tricolor*, are usually sold as a mixture of hybrids in garden centres and shops. These come in a wide range of colours from white through yellow and orange to red, most having a striking throat in a contrasting colour separated by a dark band.

Sparaxis can be grown outside in warm, sheltered positions in areas where the temperature seldom falls below freezing, but will need a protective mulch of bark or leafmould which should be removed in mid-spring. To ensure success it is usually better to plant in mid-spring and then lift the corms after the first frost has blackened the foliage storing them in a cool, dry place.

In other areas they are best grown as pot plants either moved to a warm, sunny patio when in flower or kept permanently in greenhouses and conservatories. For these situations they can be planted in autumn for late spring and early summer flowers or in spring for flowers in late summer. Keep the compost fairly dry until growth starts, then water more frequently when in growth. Feed regularly with a liquid fertilizer when in growth. Stop watering when the foliage starts to die down and keep the compost dry until growth starts again.

The flowers can be cut for indoor decoration.

Plants can be propagated by removing offsets in spring or autumn.

soil	Sparaxis needs a well-drained soil or compost for best results
site	Site in a position in full sun outside or in good light indoors
planting	Plant corms 5cm (2in) deep and space them roughly 10cm (4in) apart
general care	Keep plants reasonably well watered when in growth, but stop watering as the foliage starts to wither
pests & disease	Relatively trouble free. Pests and diseases do not usually cause any problems to this plant

Sparaxis tricolor

	SPRING	SUMMER	AUTUMN	WINTER	height (cm)	spread (cm)	flower colour	
Sparaxis elegans					20	10		Good for sunny rockeries
S. tricolor					30	10		Usually sold as mixed hybrids

 planting ⚹ flowering

Bulbs S

Sternbergia

Autumn daffodil

BULB

A beautiful plant for brightening up the garden in autumn, although the flowers look more like a crocus than they do to the closely related daffodil. It is a little fussy in its requirements, but well worth growing.

Although the genus contains a number of species, only *Sternbergia lutea* is reliable and regularly grown. *S. sicula* (sometimes listed as *S. lutea* subsp. *sicula*) is similar in its needs, is much shorter with narrower leaves but is not commonly available. *S. lutea* produces its goblet-shaped flowers shortly after the strap-shaped, dark green basal leaves emerge in autumn.

Plants need a warm, dry summer dormancy, from mid- to late summer, to flower well the following season in early to mid-autumn and are best planted close to a warm wall, on a warm rock garden or similar sheltered position away from cold winds. They particularly like alkaline soils, especially those that are well drained.

They can also be planted at the front of borders providing they can be left undisturbed to build up large and congested clumps. Make sure that other plants growing around them do not grow over them so that they become shaded in summer as this will discourage flowering.

Feeding with sulphate of potash in autumn and early spring will help ripen the bulbs and encourage flowering.

Plants dislike disturbance but overcrowded clumps can be lifted and divided when dormant, especially when flowering is reduced.

soil	For best results, plant Sternbergia in an extremely well-drained soil
site	These plants require a warm, sheltered position in full sun
planting	Plant the bulbs 10cm (4in) deep and space them roughly 10cm (4in) apart
general care	For general care of these plants, keep the soil dry in summer to ensure reliable flowering in autumn
pests & disease	Relatively trouble free. Pests and diseases do not usually cause any problems to this plant

Sternbergia lutea

S

Bulbs

Tecophilaea

Chilean blue
crocus
CORM

If there is one bulbous plant that gets the hearts of plant lovers racing, then it has to be the Chilean blue crocus – the flowers are large and a wonderful almost electric blue. Although the plants are small and only produce one or two narrow leaves, the flowers measuring 3cm (1¼in) across are large in comparison and face upwards.

soil	Grow in a gritty, loam-based compost indoors or a well-drained, sandy soil outside
site	Brightly lit with some direct sunlight indoors, or a sheltered position in full sun outside
planting	Plant 5cm (2in) deep; 10cm (4in) apart or three corms per 12.5cm (5in) pot
general care	Generally, care and maintenance for these plants is fairly easy. Give light liquid feeds every fortnight when in growth
pests & disease	Usually trouble free from pests and diseases, but narcissus fly and basal rot can be a problem

Due to extensive wild plant collection in the past this plant is now an endangered species, so growing it at home should help ensure its survival. This fact has also made the corms expensive to buy – however, the end result is well worth the initial outlay.

Tecophilaea is hardy and can be grown outside in a warm position in very well-drained soil, but it is far better to treat it as an indoor plant for a frost-free greenhouse – having paid for the corms the last thing you want is for the plants to die! Another reason for growing under glass is that the foliage emerges early in the year and may be susceptible to frosts. Because of its size it needs careful placement outdoors to prevent it being swamped by other plants, but looks very good in association with short silver-leaved plants. After planting outside, cover the soil with grit for extra protection.

When growing in pots, water only when plants are in growth, reducing water gradually after flowering. When dormant keep the compost almost but not completely dry. Withholding water in winter can delay leaf emergence, if need be, until the weather becomes a little warmer.

Plants can be propagated by removing offsets when repotting or replanting.

Tecophilaea cyanocrocus

	SPRING	SUMMER	AUTUMN	WINTER	height (cm)	spread (cm)	flower colour	
Tecophilaea cyanocrocus	● ●		✎ ✎		10	8		Flowers have a paler centre
T. cyanocrocus 'Leichtlinii'	● ●		✎ ✎		10	8		Flowers have a prominent white centre
T. cyanocrocus 'Violacea'	● ●		✎ ✎		10	8		Not as interesting

 planting flowering

Bulbs

T

Tigridia
Tiger flower
BULB

The brightly coloured flowers of this plant get their common name from the colourful dark red or purple markings on the smaller inner petals and throat. The spectacular flowers only last for a day, but plants can produce plenty of blooms over several months from mid-summer to early autumn.

The iris-like flowers of *Tigridia pavonia*, the commonest species available, look exotic and measure approximately 10cm (4in) across. They can be yellow, orange, red, pink or white in colour. Several are produced in succession on a central flower stem that arises from the fan of erect, pleated leaves. Plants can reach roughly 45cm (18in) in height.

The bulbs should be planted in spring, preferably mid- to late spring after the fear of frosts has passed, in a warm, sunny, sheltered position that can offer protection from cold or strong winds. Add plenty of compost at planting time, and a good dressing of sharp sand or grit where the soil is heavy.

Originating from South America, the tiger flower is not frost hardy and so the bulbs should be lifted in autumn when the

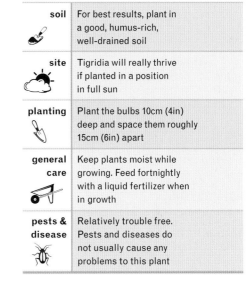

soil	For best results, plant in a good, humus-rich, well-drained soil
site	Tigridia will really thrive if planted in a position in full sun
planting	Plant the bulbs 10cm (4in) deep and space them roughly 15cm (6in) apart
general care	Keep plants moist while growing. Feed fortnightly with a liquid fertilizer when in growth
pests & disease	Relatively trouble free. Pests and diseases do not usually cause any problems to this plant

leaves have withered, dried and then stored in just damp sand at a temperature of 8–12°C (45–55°F). In warm regions with dry winters and light frosts they can be kept in the ground all year, but are best protected by a thick mulch of bark or similar insulating material.

Alternatively, for best results, the bulbs can be planted in pots of loam-based compost and planted out in the garden in early summer. Or they can be grown to provide beautiful permanent displays in cool greenhouses and conservatories. In the latter case stop watering as the leaves start to die down; the bulbs can then be overwintered in the dry compost and repotted into fresh compost in spring.

The tiger flower is usually sold as a mixture of hybrids in a range of various colours.

Plants can be propagated from offsets removed in autumn; they generally take two to three years to reach flowering size.

Tigridia pavonia

T

Bulbs

Trillium
Wood lily *or* Wake robin
Rʜɪᴢᴏᴍᴇ

A fabulous plant for shady and woodland conditions especially when planted in large groups or allowed to spread so their foliage provides ground cover. White-flowered forms help brighten up dull areas.

Trillium grandiflorum

T. chloropetalum var. giganteum

The tri- part of the name – Trillium – gives the clue that everything about the wood lilies comes in threes. The stems are topped by three broad leaves and a single flower with three small sepals and three large petals. The flowers can measure up to 9cm (3½in) across in *Trillium chloropetalum*, but are more usually 5–6cm (2-2½in) across.

The leaves can be up to 20cm (8in) long and in some species, such as *T. chloropetalum*, *T. luteum*, *T. recurvatum* and *T. rivale*, they have attractive markings. Although they are all hardy, the foliage of *T. rivale* can be damaged by late frosts.

Plants need some shade above and humus-rich moist soil below. Dig in plenty of leafmould, composted bark or compost before planting together with gritty sand in poorly drained soils. In these conditions they soon become established to produce large clumps. Initially they are slow to establish and once settled resent root disturbance.

Apart from woodland gardens, trilliums can also be grown in cool, peaty gardens and rock gardens. They will not scorch in full sun providing the roots are supplied with plenty of moisture.

They can also be grown in pots in a cold greenhouse where their flowers can be appreciated close up, and where they will also be protected from rain splash.

Plants are propagated by lifting and dividing the rhizomes in autumn and replanting immediately.

Trillium erectum f. albiflorum

soil	Needs a well-drained, humus-rich, moisture-retentive soil that is lime free
site	These plants will grow well in a position in partial to moderate shade
planting	Plant rhizomes 7.5–10cm (3–4in) deep and space them roughly 30cm (12in) apart
general care	Dig in leafmould or some other compost when planting. Mulch plants in spring to maintain soil humus and moisture levels
pests & disease	Slugs and snails may be a problem, but otherwise these are relatively trouble free from pests and diseases

	SPRING	SUMMER	AUTUMN	WINTER	height (cm)	spread (cm)	flower colour	
Trillium chloropetalum	● ●				45	45		Flowers can be white, greenish-white, yellow or maroon
T. chloropetalum var. giganteum	● ●				45	45		Robust form with mottled foliage
T. erectum	● ●				40	30		Pale green foliage
T. grandiflorum		● ●			45	45		Flowers turn pink as they age
T. grandiflorum 'Flore Pleno'		● ●			45	45		Double flowers
T. luteum	● ●				40	30		Foliage blotched dark bronze-green
T. recurvatum	● ●				40	30		Foliage mottled bronze
T. rivale	● ●				15	10		Flowers often flushed pink with purple-pink spotting

planting   ● flowering

Bulbs

Triteleia
CORM

The triteleias bear clusters of many colourful funnel-shaped flowers in summer amid sparse foliage that will not get in the way of other plants. The flowers are produced in loose clusters of around 20 flowers up to 5cm (2in) long, similar to Allium flowers.

Triteleia laxa 'Koningin Fabiola'

Triteleia flowers are good for cutting to use in indoor arrangements.

The plants tolerate temperatures down to -5°C (23°F) and can be grown in warm borders – especially at the base of a sunny wall, on rock gardens and in containers. Plants may need protection with a mulch of bark chips in autumn in cold regions. Because of their sparse foliage they should be planted together in bold groups for the best displays.

Plants will grow reliably where they can receive plenty of moisture when growing, followed by a warm, dry period when dormant in late summer and early autumn.

If your soil is heavy or you cannot provide a sheltered position, then the plants will do much better if grown in pots of loam-based compost with added grit for drainage. Keep the pots in a cool, but frost-free place – such as plunged in sand inside a cool, but frost-free coldframe or sheltered position outside or in a cold greenhouse – with plenty of light until the shoots begin to appear when they can be brought indoors.

Previously, plants were classified within the Brodiaea family and are often still listed as such in books and catalogues.

Plants dislike disturbance but are propagated by dividing clumps or removing offsets in autumn; the offsets usually take two years to flower.

soil	For best results, plant Triteleia in any light, well-drained soil
site	These plants need to be planted in an open, sheltered, sunny position
planting	Plant corms 7.5cm (3in) deep and space them roughly 10cm (4in) apart
general care	Feed with a high potash liquid fertilizer early summer. Remove faded flowers; allow foliage to die back before removing
pests & disease	Relatively trouble free. Pests and diseases do not usually cause any problems to this plant

Triteleia laxa

	SPRING	SUMMER	AUTUMN	WINTER	height (cm)	spread (cm)	flower colour
Triteleia hyacinthina	●	●			45	15	☐ Flowers may be pale blue
T. laxa		● ●			45	15	☐ Flowers may be white
T. laxa 'Koningin Fabiola'		● ●			50	15	☐ Flowers up to 5cm long

 planting   flowering

Bulbs

T

Tritonia
CORM

Tritonias are grown for their colourful trumpet or funnel-shaped blooms which are best appreciated when grown in pots for indoor displays. The flowers are up to 5cm (2in) wide and produced in groups of up to 10 on wiry stems above the flattish fans of sword-shaped leaves.

Tritonia disticha subsp. *rubrolucens*

Although both Tritonia species are best grown indoors, *Tritonia disticha* subsp. *rubrolucens* can be grown outside in areas where the winter temperature rarely drops much below freezing. The corms will need to be planted in a warm position, preferably at the base of a sunny wall.

The soil should be treated to a thick mulch of bark chips in the autumn which is removed in late spring when the danger of further severe frosts has passed.

soil	Tritonia needs a well-drained, humus-rich soil or loam-free compost
site	Requires a warm, sheltered position outdoors or a position in good light indoors
planting	Plant corms 5cm (2in) deep and space them roughly 10–15cm (4–6in) apart
general care	Generally easy to cultivate. Remove faded flowerheads and foliage when the plant dies down
pests & disease	Relatively trouble free. Pests and diseases do not usually cause any problems to this plant

Tritonia crocata

For growing indoors plant five or six corms in a 15cm (6in) pot of compost. Do not water until the leaves appear unless the compost starts to dry out. Maintain a minimum temperature of 7–10°C (45–50°F). Keep the compost moist and feed fortnightly with a liquid fertilizer when the plants are growing. Plants will probably need staking with split bamboo canes. Continue watering until the leaves start to turn yellow (this will take place in the summer for *T. crocata* and during the winter for *T. disticha*), then allow the compost to dry out. The corms can be left in the pots for two years but are best repotted annually.

Plants are propagated by carefully removing offsets at planting time. Grow these on in pots to flower in two to three years' time.

Tritonia disticha subsp. *rubrolucens*

	SPRING	SUMMER	AUTUMN	WINTER	height (cm)	spread (cm)	flower colour	
Tritonia crocata	● ●		✿ ✿		45	8		Flowers may be white or pink
T. disticha subsp. *rubrolucens*	✿ ✿		● ●		60	10		Hardier than *T. crocata*

✿ planting ● flowering

Tropaeolum

Perennial
nasturtium

RHIZOME, TUBER

The perennial nasturtiums are versatile plants, with colourful flowers and attractive foliage, which can be trained as climbers or allowed to sprawl across the ground for ground cover or scramble through other plants.

The Tropaeolum flowers have long spurs and the foliage is deeply lobed. *Tropaeolum polyphyllum* and *T. speciosum* produce rhizomes, *T. tuberosum* produces tubers.

T. polyphyllum is the hardiest, surviving down to -15°C (5°F) providing it is grown in well-drained soil, such as a raised bed where it will trail elegantly over the edge.

T. tuberosum needs a frost-free position, although it will survive short-lived light frosts especially if the soil is mulched in autumn. The tubers are best lifted in autumn and stored in just moist compost in cool but frost-free, dry conditions and replanted in spring. *T.* 'Ken Aslet' is more reliable than the species as it flowers earlier and so is a better choice for cool regions. *T. tuberosum* can also be grown in a cool greenhouse or conservatory.

soil	For best results, plant in any light, well-drained, humus-rich soil
site	Most prefer a position in full sun, although *T. speciosum* prefers the shade
planting	Plant 2.5cm (1in) deep, setting rhizomes horizontally; space them 30cm (12in) apart
general care	Mulch the soil in spring and in autumn. Remove the dead foliage in autumn before mulching
pests & disease	Aphids may be a problem, but otherwise pests and diseases do not usually cause any problems to this plant

T. speciosum, on the other hand, prefers cool, moist conditions and a position in light shade – especially around the roots and lower stem otherwise it can be difficult to establish. Once it gets going it can become rampant and looks good growing through dark-leaved conifers and on shady walls.

Plants with rhizomes can be easily propagated by dividing the rhizomes in spring before growth starts. *T. tuberosum* can be propagated from small tubers when replanting.

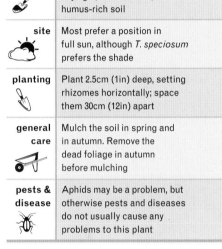

Tropaeolum speciosum

	SPRING	SUMMER	AUTUMN	WINTER	height (cm)	spread (cm)	flower colour	
Tropaeolum polyphyllum	planting	flowering			10	60		Grey-green foliage
T. speciosum	planting	flowering	flowering		300	60		Blue-green foliage. Sometimes produces blue berries
T. tuberosum	planting		flowering		300	60		Greyish green foliage with purplish stems
T. tuberosum var. *lineamaculatum* 'Ken Aslet'	planting	flowering	flowering		250	60		Blue-green foliage

 planting   flowering

Tulbaghia

Wild garlic *or*
Society garlic
CORM

Tulbaghias are grown for their dainty looking star-like flowers that are nonetheless remarkably sturdy produced at the end of slender stems. The flowers are up to 2.5cm (1in) across and produced in groups of up to 20.

The flowers of *Tulbaghia simmleri* (sometimes listed under its old name *T. fragrans*) are very fragrant, but you have to go out in the late evening to enjoy the scent. Tulbaghia leaves are long and narrow and in *T. violacea* smell of garlic when crushed. Plants produce vigorous clumps when fully established.

Plants are not completely hardy, surviving temperatures down to -5°C

soil	Needs a well-drained, humus-rich light soil or loam-based compost
site	Tulbaghia needs to have a position where it receives the full sun
planting	Plant corms 2.5–5cm (1–2in) deep and space them 20–25cm (8–10in) apart
general care	Generally these plants are easy to care for. Apply a slow-release fertilizer in spring. Remove faded flowerheads
pests & disease	Relatively trouble free. Pests and diseases do not usually cause any problems to this plant

Tulbaghia simmleri

(23°F), but can be grown at the front of sunny borders or on rock gardens or, better still, at the bottom of a sunny wall. A deep winter mulch will help ensure survival from severe frosts.

It is usually better to grow the plants inside as houseplants or in a cool greenhouse or conservatory in good sized containers. Indoors plants will often flower for much longer than when grown outside. Water regularly when plants are in growth, reducing the water as the flower spikes emerge and again as plants become dormant. Plants will need a minimum temperature of 5°C (40°F).

Plants can be propagated by dividing the established plants in the spring.

Tulbaghia violacea

	SPRING	SUMMER	AUTUMN	WINTER	height (cm)	spread (cm)	flower colour	
Tulbaghia simmleri	planting	• •			60	30		Produces grey-green foliage
T. violacea	planting	•	• •		60	30		Semi-evergreen mid-green to bluish-green foliage
T. violacea 'Silver Lace'	planting	• •	• •		50	30		Produces cream striped foliage

planting   • flowering

Bulbs

T

128

Tulipa
Tulip
BULB

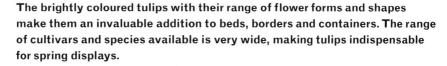

The brightly coloured tulips with their range of flower forms and shapes make them an invaluable addition to beds, borders and containers. The range of cultivars and species available is very wide, making tulips indispensable for spring displays.

Tulipa 'Stresa'

The flowers range in colour from white through yellow, orange and pink or red through to deep purple and even green. Many have splashes or streaks of contrasting colours. There are singles as well as double-flowered forms.

There are suitable choices for the rock garden, in informal groups in beds and borders or in formal bedding schemes as well as growing in containers including forcing for indoor displays.

Like daffodils, tulips are split into a number of divisions to make classification

Tulipa 'Ballerina'

of the different cultivars easier.

Division 1 Single early tulips. Single, cup-shaped flowers, usually starting to flower in mid-spring.

Division 2 Double early tulips. Double, fully double flowers, usually starting to flower in mid-spring.

Tulipa 'Apricot Beauty'

Tulipa 'China Pink'

soil	Tulips need a well-drained, humus-rich soil to achieve best results
site	These plants grow well if given a position in full sun
planting	Plant 10–25cm deep depending on size/soil conditions; 10–20cm apart depending on height
general care	Bulbs bruise easily. Feed with high potash granular fertilizer in late winter/early spring. Water freely during dry spells when in growth
pests & disease	Aphids, slugs and tulip fire disease may be a problem. Apart from these, tulips are fairly trouble free

T

Bulbs

Tulipa 'Fancy Frills'

Tulipa 'Orange Princess'

Tulipa 'Olympic Flame'

Division 3 Triumph tulips. Single flowers, conical at first then rounded. Mid-season flowering.

Division 4 Darwin hybrid tulips. Large, rounded, single flowers produced late spring.

Division 5 Single late tulips. Large, square or rounded single flowers produced in late spring. Includes those originally known as Darwin tulips and cottage tulips.

Division 6 Lily-flowered tulips. Single flowers with long pointed petals often reflexed at their tips produced in late spring.

Division 7 Fringed tulips. Single flowers with petals that are finely fringed at their edge produced in late spring.

Division 8 Viridiflora tulips. Single flowers with petals with broad green marks on the outside of the petals produced in late spring.

Division 9 Rembrandt tulips. Large, single flowers with colour breaks, produced by viruses, with streaks and splashes of a contrasting colour produced in late spring.

Division 10 Parrot tulips. Very large, single flowers with deeply frilled and wavy petals produced in late spring.

Division 11 Double late tulips. Large, fully double flowers produced in late spring; often referred to as 'paeony-flowered' tulips.

	SPRING	SUMMER	AUTUMN	WINTER	height (cm)	spread (cm)	flower colour	
Tulipa 'Angelique'	●			✂	40	15	▦	Division 11
T. 'Apricot Beauty'	● ●			✂	35	15	▤	Division 1
T. 'Aristocrat'	● ●			✂	50	20	▥	Division 5
T. 'Artist'	●			✂	45	20	▥	Division 8
T. 'Ballerina'	●			✂	55	20	▦	Division 6
T. 'Black Parrot'	● ●			✂	50	20	▦	Division 10
T. 'China Pink'				✂	50	20	▢	Division 6
T. 'Early Harvest'	●			✂	20	10	▦	Division 12
T. 'Esperanto'	●			✂	35	15	▥	Division 8
T. 'Fancy Frills'	●			✂	45	15	▦	Division 7

 planting   flowering

Tulipa 'Monte Carlo'

Tulipa 'Prinses Irene'

Tulipa 'Oxford'

Division 12 Kaufmanniana hybrid tulips. Flowers with strap-shaped petals opening flat and giving rise to the common name of waterlily tulips, opening in early spring. Derived from *T. kaufmanniana*.

Division 13 Fosteriana hybrid tulips. Oval to oblong flowers which generally open widely produced in mid-spring. Derived from *T. fosteriana*.

Division 14 Greigii hybrid tulips. Derived from *T. greigii* and normally having brown-purple mottled foliage and flowers produced in early to mid-spring.

Division 15 Miscellaneous. Numerous species and their selections and hybrids.

The single early tulips are sturdy and fairly weather resistant. The double early tulips also have sturdy stems, are long flowering and good for cutting. Darwin hybrid tulips are the best choice for bedding schemes. The parrot and double late tulips are not very weather-resistant and either

	SPRING	SUMMER	AUTUMN	WINTER	height (cm)	spread (cm)	flower colour	
T. 'Fantasy'	● ●			✂	50	20		Division 10
T. 'Fringed Beauty'	●			✂	35	15		Division 7
T. 'Garden Party'	● ●			✂	45	15		Division 3
T. 'Jewel of Spring'	● ●			✂	50	15		Division 4
T. 'Keizerskroon'	●			✂	30	10		Division 1
T. linifolia (Batalinii Group) 'Bright Gem'	●			✂	15	8		Division 15
T. 'Little Beauty'	●			✂	10	5		Division 15
T. 'Monte Carlo'	●			✂	40	10		Division 2
T. 'Olympic Flame'	● ●			✂	45	10		Division 4
T. 'Orange Bouquet'	●			✂	50	15		Division 3
T. 'Orange Emperor'	● ●			✂	40	10		Division 13
T. 'Orange Princess'				✂	35	10		Division 11
T. 'Oranje Nassau'	●			✂	30	10		Division 2
T. 'Oratorio'	● ●			✂	20	8		Division 14
T. 'Oxford'	● ●			✂	50	15		Division 4

✂ planting   ● flowering

Tulipa 'Toronto'

Tulipa turkestanica

need a sheltered site or are grown in containers under cover. When grown in favourable conditions the flowers are long lasting and are good for cutting. The hybrids in divisions 12, 13 and 14 are usually short in stature and make good choices for rock gardens and containers, although the division 14 cultivars are somewhat taller.

In the wild, tulips grow on open rocky sun-baked hills which means they need plenty of light and a fairly warm, dry period in summer when dormant. The soil is usually alkaline, so add garden lime to acid soils. If the soil is heavy clay, add grit or sharp sand before planting and plant large bulbs roughly 15cm (6in) deep.

Because the dormant bulbs need warm, dry conditions they can be lifted in summer, once the foliage has died down, and stored in trays in a dry place out of direct sunlight to ripen until re-planting in autumn. Those used in bedding schemes are usually lifted to make room for summer displays.

When grown in informal groups in mixed borders the bulbs can be left alone and will usually perform well for several years providing the site is warm and dry, and the dormant bulbs are not overshadowed by too much foliage. Even these will benefit from lifting every four to five years. Some of the

Tulipa 'Purissima'

Tulipa 'Spring Green'

species tulips are less long lived and should be lifted or, better still, grown in pots that can be stored in warmth in the summer. The dwarf species are best grown in a rock garden, raised bed or at the front of borders, as well as planted in pots for an attractive display.

Plants can be propagated by removing offsets at lifting time. They will take a couple of years to reach flowering size.

Bulbs

	SPRING	SUMMER	AUTUMN	WINTER	height (cm)	spread (cm)	flower colour	
T. 'Plaisir'	●			✿	15	5	▦	Division 14
T. praestans 'Fusilier'	● ●			✿	30	10	▦	Division 15
T. 'Prinses Irene'	●			✿	35	10	▦	Division 3
T. 'Purissima'	● ●			✿	35	10	▢	Division 13
T. 'Red Riding Hood'	●			✿	20	8	▦	Division 14
T. 'Spring Green'	●			✿	40	15	▦	Division 8
T. 'Stockholm'	●			✿	30	10	▦	Division 2
T. 'Stresa'	●			✿	15	5	▦	Division 12
T. 'Sweet Harmony'	● ●			✿	50	20	▦	Division 5
T. 'Toronto'	● ●			✿	30	10	▦	Division 14
T. turkestanica	● ●			✿	30	15	▢	Division 15
T. 'Union Jack'		●		✿	60	20	▦	Division 5
T. 'West Point'		●		✿	50	20	▦	Division 6
T. 'White Triumphator'		●		✿	70	20	▢	Division 6
T. 'Yellow Purissima'	●			✿	45	15	▦	Division 13

✿ planting   ● flowering

Uvularia

Bellwort *or*
Merry-bells
RHIZOME

The unusual but fascinating nodding flowers of Uvularia bring colour and grace to a cool, shady position in spring. The flowers measure up to 5cm (2in) long and have narrow, twisted petals. These are borne on the ends of arching stalks emerging from where the upper leaves join the stem. The lance-shaped leaves clasp the stems.

Even when the flowers have faded the ornamental stems and foliage remain fresh and attractive, resembling to some degree a dwarf bamboo.

Native of deciduous woodland in North America, uvularias are best planted on the edge of woodland, in a shady position in borders or rock gardens or even beside a pond, providing the roots are above water level and the soil does not become waterlogged. They look especially attractive when planted among ferns, other spring-flowering bulbs such as trilliums and arisaemas, and herbaceous perennials such as polemoniums.

When first planting the rhizomes, improve the soil by digging in plenty of lime-free compost, leafmould or other similar materials.

The two species of Uvularia listed below produce large clumps when established. Plants are propagated by dividing the clumps in autumn or early spring.

soil	Needs a well-drained, moisture-retentive, humus-rich preferably lime-free soil
site	Uvularia enjoys a position where there is some or partial shade
planting	Plant rhizomes 2.5–5cm (1–2in) deep and space them roughly 20–25cm (8–10in) apart
general care	Mulch the soil with an acidic mulch in spring to help improve humus content
pests & disease	Slugs and snails may be a problem. Apart from these, Uvularia is relatively trouble free

Uvularia grandiflora

	SPRING	SUMMER	AUTUMN	WINTER	height (cm)	spread (cm)	flower colour
Uvularia grandiflora	🌱 ● ● ●			🌱	60	30	Bright green foliage
U. perfoliata	🌱	● ●		🌱	45	30	Greyish-green foliage

 planting   *flowering*

Veltheimia

BULB

The curious tubular flowers of veltheimias – resembling a red hot poker – are produced over several weeks in winter and make this plant invaluable for indoor colour at this otherwise gloomy time of year.

The waxy pink flowers, up to 4cm (1½in) long, hang in densely packed spikes (up to 10cm/4in long) of up to 60 flowers at the top of a strong upright stem. Even when they are not in flower, the rosettes of bold, glossy, wavy-edged leaves, which are up to 30cm (12in) long, are decorative in their own right.

Hailing from South Africa, the two species of Veltheimia need a minimum winter temperature of 5°C (41°F) and can be displayed on bright windowsills or in cool greenhouses or conservatories.

Pot up the bulbs individually in 12.5–15cm (5–6in) pots. After planting keep the compost reasonably moist until the shoots appear, allowing the surface of the compost to dry before watering again. Then water and feed regularly when in active growth. Stop watering and feeding when the leaves start to turn yellow, and keep the compost dry to provide a dormancy period of about eight weeks in summer. Start watering again when new growth appears.

Disturbing the roots will inhibit flowering and plants only need repotting when flowering becomes impaired. Instead, simply scrape away the top 2.5cm (1in) or so of compost and replace with fresh.

Plants are propagated by removing offsets when the bulbs are dormant or at potting time.

Veltheimia bracteata

soil	Veltheimia will perform well if grown in a loam-based compost
site	Needs a position in good light that receives some direct sunlight
planting	Plant with tip of the bulb level with the compost surface, one bulb per 12.5–15cm (5–6in) pot
general care	Generally, care and maintenance for these plants is straightforward. Cut off the flower stems as the flowers fade
pests & disease	Relatively trouble free. Pests and diseases do not usually cause any problems to this plant

	SPRING	SUMMER	AUTUMN	WINTER	height (cm)	spread (cm)	flower colour	
Veltheimia bracteata	●		✎	● ●	45	30		Flowers sometimes tinged yellow
V. capensis	●		✎	●	40	30		Flowers have pale green tips

✎ planting   ● flowering

Bulbs

Watsonia

CORM

Watsonias are attractive, half-hardy plants that provide summer colour. There are numerous species, most of which are only stocked by specialists – but when you see them offered, get your hands on some.

The elegant, upright spikes of flowers, not unlike those of Gladiolus, make the South African Watsonia perfect for growing in sunny borders – especially when associated with grey-leaved plants.

Each stem carries a branching spike of tubular flowers, up to 5cm (2in) long, that open into a star shape on either side of the stem. Some species produce very tall flower spikes that will benefit from staking. The foliage, produced along the stem and at the base of the plant, is narrow, upright and sword-like.

The corms can be planted directly outside from mid-spring or potted up and grown on in a cool greenhouse for planting out from late spring after frosts.

In mild areas where it rarely falls to -5°C (34°F), the corms may be left in the ground over winter providing the soil is well mulched with bark chippings or similar; remove the mulch in spring as the shoots appear. Otherwise, lift the corms after the foliage has died down, dry them in a warm place for a day or two and store them in dry sand or compost in a cool, but frost-free, dry place. Late summer and autumn flowering species are more or less evergreen and should not be dried out.

Plants are propagated by removing offsets in spring or at lifting time.

soil	For best results, plant in any well-drained, light soil or good compost
site	Needs to be positioned in good light indoors or a warm, sunny situation outside
planting	Plant corms 10cm (4in) deep and space them roughly 20–25cm (8–10in) apart
general care	Feed with a slow-release fertilizer in spring. Water during prolonged dry periods. Remove faded flowers and dead foliage
pests & disease	Aphids and thrips can be a problem, but usually trouble free from most other pests and diseases

Watsonia pillansii

	SPRING		SUMMER		AUTUMN	WINTER	height (cm)	spread (cm)	flower colour	
Watsonia borbonica	🛠	🛠	●	●			120	45		Flowers are slightly scented
W. pillansii	🛠	🛠	●	●			100	40		Flowers may be orange-red
W. 'Tresco Dwarf Pink'	🛠	🛠	●	●			35	15		Reasonably hardy

 planting   *flowering*

Zantedeschia

Arum lily *or*
Calla lily

RHIZOME

These bold, large flowered plants produce spectacular displays in either the garden or cool greenhouse or conservatory, depending on their hardiness. The hardier plants look elegant and dramatic when planted near or in water.

soil	For best results, plant in any moist, humus-rich soil or a loam-based compost
site	Zantedeschias prefer to be planted in a warm and sunny position
planting	Plant rhizomes 10–15cm (4–6in) deep and space them roughly 40–45cm (16–18in) apart
general care	Keep plants moist. Mulch the crowns of outdoor plants in late autumn to protect them against frost
pests & disease	Leaf spot disease can be a problem, but usually trouble free from most other pests and diseases

Arum lilies produce large flowers comprising a spathe and spadix (see p33); the spathe can be up to 28cm (11in) long and are much prized by flower arrangers as they make good cut flowers. The large arrow-shaped foliage is attractive in its own right and also used for floral decoration.

The hardier *Zantedeschia aethiopica* and its cultivars will survive down to -10°C (14°F) and can be grown outside. Add lots of well-rotted manure or compost to the soil when planting. It makes an excellent focal point in cool,

Zantedeschia aethiopica 'Crowborough'

shady borders, bog gardens, large containers and even as a marginal aquatic plant as long as the water does not freeze. In the latter case, plant the rhizomes in aquatic baskets and place at a depth of 15–30cm (6–12in).

Z. elliottiana and *Z. rehmannii* will tolerate temperatures down to -4°C (25°F) for short periods, but are best grown in pots as a cool greenhouse or conservatory plant. Plants can also be brought outside in late spring or early summer, then moved inside again in autumn. Even *Z. aethiopica* benefits from overwintering in a frost-free greenhouse or conservatory when grown in pots as the rhizomes will be damaged if the compost freezes.

Containerized plants should be watered and fed regularly when in growth, but reduce watering in late summer. Outside the foliage is likely to be cut down by frosts, but indoors may remain evergreen through winter and the compost will need to be kept just moist if this is the case.

Plants are propagated by lifting and dividing the rhizomes in spring.

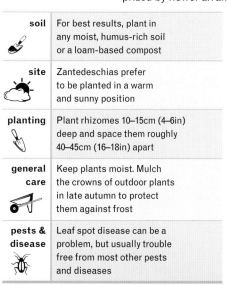

Zantedeschia aethiopica

Bulbs

	SPRING	SUMMER	AUTUMN	WINTER	height (cm)	spread (cm)	flower colour	
Zantedeschia aethiopica	🌱 🌱 🌱	● ● ●			100	50	☐	Flowers have a yellow centre
Z. aethiopica 'Crowborough'	🌱 🌱 🌱	● ● ●			90	45	☐	Hardier than the species
Z. aethiopica 'Green Goddess'	🌱 🌱 🌱	● ● ●			90	45	▨	Flowers have a pale green throat
Z. 'Black Eyed Beauty'	🌱 🌱 🌱	● ● ●			60	40	☐	Flowers have a black eye
Z. elliottiana	🌱 🌱 🌱	● ●			75	30	▨	Not hardy
Z. rehmannii	🌱 🌱 🌱	● ●			80	30	☐	Not hardy

🌱 planting   ● flowering

Zephyranthes

Zephyr lily
BULB

The beautiful zephyr lily bears crocus-like flowers mainly in autumn. Only one species can be grown outside the others are best treated as houseplants or grown in cool conservatories or greenhouses.

The upturned flowers can measure up to 5cm (2in) wide and are produced singly at the top of the stems which usually appear before the leaves which are dark green, narrow and rush-like. The foliage of *Zephyranthes candida* is virtually evergreen.

Only *Z. candida* is hardy enough to grow outside, tolerating temperatures down to -5°C (23°F). It needs to be grown in a warm, sunny site either at the front of a border or, better still, at the base of a sunny, warm wall, which will help provide winter protection. Plants will need a thick mulch in autumn to protect against frost and will

soil	Needs a well-drained, humus-rich, light soil or a loam-based compost
site	Prefers to be sited in a sheltered position in full sun
planting	Plant 10cm (4in) deep, 10cm (4in) apart outside; in pots, 5cm (2in) deep, six bulbs per 15cm (6in) pot
general care	Water well when in active growth, keeping the soil or compost damp especially during prolonged warm, dry periods
pests & disease	Relatively trouble free. Pests and diseases do not usually cause any problems to this plant

Zephyranthes candida

benefit from being covered with a cloche to protect against rain. *Z. rosea* can be grown outside in mild regions but the bulbs should be lifted in autumn and stored in a cool, dry, frost-free place.

The other frost-tender species, including *Z. candida* where cold winters would be a problem, are best grown in pots. Keep the compost just moist until growth starts, then water and feed regularly when plants are in growth. Stop watering and feeding when the foliage starts to turn yellow and keep the compost just dry – not bone dry – during the dormant period.

Plants flower better when they are potbound, so only repot when the pots become congested. Instead, scrape off the top 2.5cm (1in) or so of compost annually and replace with fresh.

Plants can be propagated by removing offsets in late spring.

	SPRING	SUMMER	AUTUMN	WINTER	height (cm)	spread (cm)	flower colour
Zephyranthes candida	🌱 🌱		● ● ●		20	8	Flowers often have a pink tint
Z. flavissima	🌱 🌱		● ●		20	8	Needs lime-free soil
Z. rosea	🌱 🌱		● ●		30	10	Flowers have a white eye

 planting   *flowering*

Troubleshooting

The following diagram is designed to help you diagnose conditions suffered by your plants from the symptoms you can observe. Starting with the part of the plant that appears to be most affected, by answering successive questions 'yes' [✓] or 'no' [✗] you will quickly arrive at a probable cause. Once you have identified the cause, turn to the relevant entry in the directory of pests and diseases for how to treat the problem.

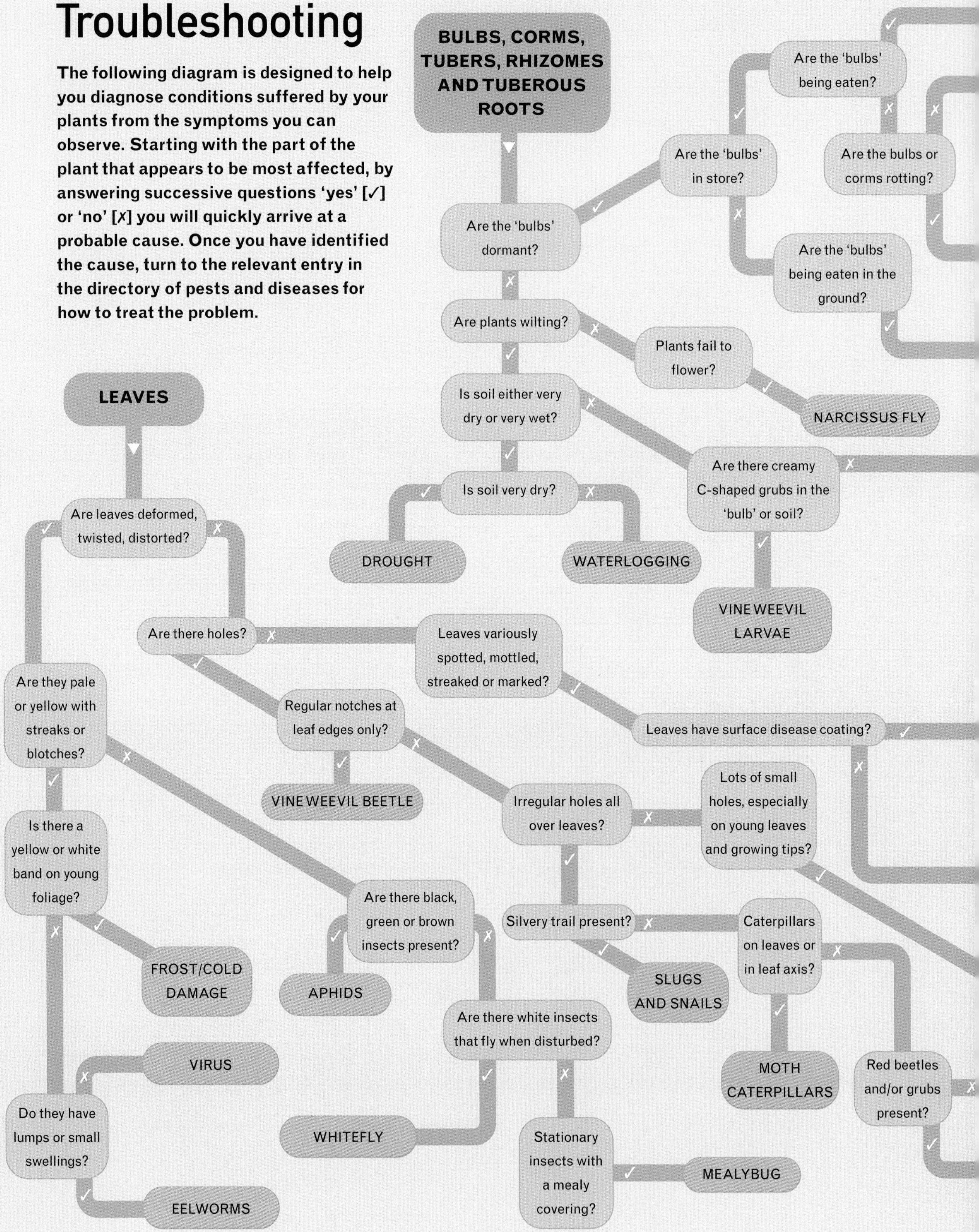

BULBS, CORMS, TUBERS, RHIZOMES AND TUBEROUS ROOTS

Are the 'bulbs' being eaten?

Are the 'bulbs' in store?

Are the bulbs or corms rotting?

Are the 'bulbs' dormant?

Are the 'bulbs' being eaten in the ground?

Are plants wilting?

Plants fail to flower?

Is soil either very dry or very wet?

NARCISSUS FLY

Is soil very dry?

Are there creamy C-shaped grubs in the 'bulb' or soil?

DROUGHT

WATERLOGGING

VINE WEEVIL LARVAE

LEAVES

Are leaves deformed, twisted, distorted?

Are there holes?

Leaves variously spotted, mottled, streaked or marked?

Are they pale or yellow with streaks or blotches?

Regular notches at leaf edges only?

Leaves have surface disease coating?

Lots of small holes, especially on young leaves and growing tips?

VINE WEEVIL BEETLE

Is there a yellow or white band on young foliage?

Irregular holes all over leaves?

Are there black, green or brown insects present?

Silvery trail present?

Caterpillars on leaves or in leaf axis?

FROST/COLD DAMAGE

APHIDS

SLUGS AND SNAILS

VIRUS

Are there white insects that fly when disturbed?

MOTH CATERPILLARS

Red beetles and/or grubs present?

Do they have lumps or small swellings?

WHITEFLY

Stationary insects with a mealy covering?

MEALYBUG

EELWORMS

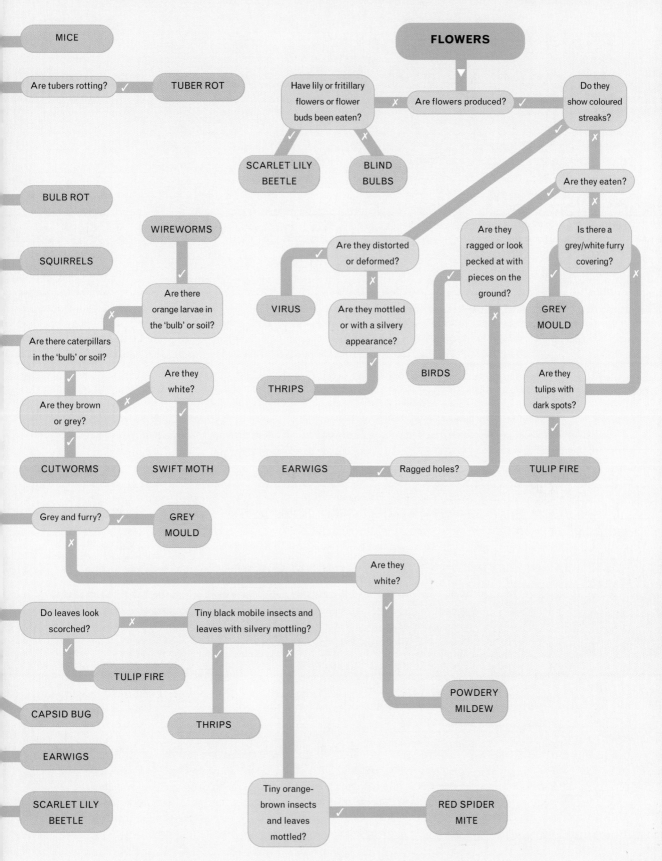

MICE

Are tubers rotting? ✓ TUBER ROT

FLOWERS

Have lily or fritillary flowers or flower buds been eaten? ✗ Are flowers produced? ✓ Do they show coloured streaks?

✓ ✗

SCARLET LILY BEETLE BLIND BULBS ✗ Are they eaten?

BULB ROT

WIREWORMS ✗ Is there a grey/white furry covering?

SQUIRRELS ✓ Are they distorted or deformed? Are they ragged or look pecked at with pieces on the ground? ✗

Are there orange larvae in the 'bulb' or soil? ✗ VIRUS ✓ GREY MOULD

Are they mottled or with a silvery appearance?

Are there caterpillars in the 'bulb' or soil? ✗ ✓ ✗

Are they white? BIRDS

Are they brown or grey? ✗ ✓ THRIPS Are they tulips with dark spots?

✓ ✓

CUTWORMS SWIFT MOTH EARWIGS ✓ Ragged holes? TULIP FIRE

Grey and furry? ✓ GREY MOULD

✗

Are they white?

Do leaves look scorched? ✗ Tiny black mobile insects and leaves with silvery mottling? ✓

✓ ✗

TULIP FIRE POWDERY MILDEW

CAPSID BUG THRIPS

EARWIGS

SCARLET LILY BEETLE Tiny orange-brown insects and leaves mottled? ✓ RED SPIDER MITE

Pests and Diseases

Many of the plants in the A-Z section are generally trouble free. Others may be attacked by one or more pests or diseases that are listed below. Growing plants in the right positions and ensuring they are as strong and healthy as possible will enable them to fend off attacks. But when they are affected immediate control will be easier to deal with, so check your plants regularly and deal with problems as soon as they occur. In addition to the insecticides listed, for a more organic approach there is a wide range of biological controls available from specialist suppliers for the control of aphids, whitefly, mealybug, red spider mite, slugs and vine weevils.

Aphids
Aphids breed quickly and a few in number can soon become a major outbreak; some will also attack the bulbs themselves. In small numbers they can easily be squashed, but when there are lots of them it might be better to spray with either a contact or systemic insecticide. Encouraging predators like ladybirds, lacewings and hoverflies is the natural method of control.

Birds, mice & squirrels
Several bird species can cause problems; sparrows especially are renowned for pecking at crocus flowers. Bird scarers such as humming lines, tin foil or CD reflectors may deter them. Both mice and squirrels will dig up and eat dormant bulbs overwintering outside in the ground or in containers. Outdoor bulbs can be protected by placing a piece of small-mesh chicken wire 2.5–5cm (1–2in) above the bulbs when planting.

Capsid bugs
A sap sucker with much larger mouthparts than aphids that tend to produce small holes with a brown edge. They can attack leaves and flowers, causing distorted growth, or young flower buds resulting in a loss of flowers. Control as for aphids.

Cutworms & wireworms
These are soil-dwelling, caterpillar-like insects that will eat the roots or bore into the underground storage organ itself. When they eat the roots plants will start to wilt no matter how much water you give them. There are no chemical control methods available. Careful hoeing around plants may kill some of the insects and expose others where they can be found by birds and other predators.

Earwigs
Earwigs are more of a nuisance than anything else, eating leaves and petals. The only method of control is to trap them. Fill a small pot with straw and suspend this upside down at flower level on a bamboo cane. Empty the pot every morning and dispose of the earwigs inside. Or you can smear the stems with petroleum jelly that the earwigs will not be able to get past.

Mealy bugs
This is a sap sucking insect that prefer to attack plants grown indoors. They cover themselves with a mealy covering that protects them against contact insecticides. Either try removing them manually or use a systemic insecticide.

Narcissus fly
The large grubs of the narcissus fly will eat bulbs in the ground. Once attacked the bulb will often rot and die. There are no chemical cures. Females lay their eggs at the tip of the bulb as the foliage is dying down, so careful hoeing around the plant to prevent entry at this time will help control them. Or try covering the bulbs with fleece pegged down at ground level after the display has finished.

Red spider mite

These tiny sap suckers are usually a problem on indoor plants but can also be a problem in hot conditions outside. They need hot, dry conditions to survive so regular misting or standing pots on trays filled with damp gravel will increase humidity and so deter them. Spray with an insecticide.

Scarlet lily beetle

These colourful beetles do a lot of damage to lilies and closely related plants such as fritillaries, and the larvae are even more voracious than the adults. As a means of defence, the larvae cover themselves with their own faeces so they resemble bird droppings. Either carefully remove the beetles and larvae by hand (early morning or evening is best) or spray the plants with a systemic insecticide.

Slugs and snails

There are numerous control methods including slug pellets, sharp, gritty barriers, traps or watering on aluminium sulphate (which also kills the eggs). Plants growing in containers can also be protected by using a 2.5cm (1in) thick barrier of petroleum jelly or copper tape on the outside rim of the pot.

Stem & bulb eelworms

If these microscopic pests attack the storage organ tell-tale dark rings can be seen when it is cut through. The leaves of affected plants are pale, twisted and have small swellings. There are no control methods so destroy affected plants and do not grow bulbs in the same place for at least three years.

Swift moth

These large, soil-dwelling caterpillars will bore large holes in underground storage organs causing great damage. There are no control methods apart from regular hoeing around the plants.

Thrips

Tiny black insects which scrape away at the outer layers of leaves and flowers, especially in hot summers. The normal symptom is a silvery flecking of the attacked areas. Control by spraying with a systemic insecticide.

Vine weevil

Both the adult beetles (see right) and the large white C-shaped grubs (see far right) will attack plants. Adults only do superficial damage but grubs feed on roots and underground storage organs. Spray plants with a systemic insecticide.

Bulb rots

There are several rots that can affect bulbs. Some will attack storage organs when they are in the ground – especially if growing in overly wet or waterlogged soils. Ensure there is adequate drainage; add sharp sand or grit to the soil. Other rotting organisms will attack the storage organ when in store indoors. Make sure they have been adequately dried before storage. If a moist storage medium is required ensure it is not too wet. Check regularly. Where signs of rot are seen cut them out and treat the cut surfaces with sulphur powder.

Grey mould (botrytis)

Grey mould will affect plants that are not growing in ideal conditions and is troublesome in cool, damp conditions. It can be a problem both indoors and out. Pick off diseased parts as soon as the fluffy mould is seen. Improve ventilation and reduce humidity around plants grown inside.

Powdery mildew

Powdery mildew attacks plants that are under stress and the disease becomes worse in hot, dry conditions. A white powdery mould develops on the surface of leaves and stems. The best method of prevention is to keep the soil or compost moist during prolonged drought periods and ensure the plants are growing strongly.

Tuber rots

Tubers may rot in the ground if conditions are too wet or waterlogged over winter. In storage, they may rot if the tubers were not dried correctly after lifting, so make sure they are dried for at least a couple of days. Diseased portions should be removed with a clean, sharp knife and the cut surface treated with sulphur.

Tulip fire

Affected plants have scorched areas on the foliage, spots on the flowers, and shoots may be covered with a velvety mould. The only control is to remove affected plants and destroy them. Do not grow tulips in the same place for at least five years.

Viruses

A number of viruses can attack bulbous plants. The leaves of those infected have distorted and stunted growth, along with yellow streaking or mottling. The only control is to remove affected plants and destroy them, as there is no effective virus control available.

Disorders

Blind bulbs

'Blind' bulbs do not produce any flowers and there are a number of causes. It could simply be that the bulbs (or offsets) are too small to flower or that the clump has become congested and it is time to lift and separate them. Attack by a pest or disease may be the problem, or that you are growing light-loving species in too much shade. Late frosts or growing tender plants in cold, exposed places may also be the reason.

Chlorosis

Chlorotic – yellow or unusually pale – leaves may be due to a basic nutrient deficiency or simply growing a lime-hater in alkaline soil. But the most likely reason is attack by pest (especially eelworms) or disease, or a cultural problem such as waterlogged soil.

Cold & frost damage

Most spring-flowering bulbs are perfectly hardy, but a sudden sharp frost can damage the new foliage as it is emerging. This usually shows up as a yellow or white band or edge to the foliage.

Forced/indoor bulbs

Unless you provide the correct conditions for forced or indoor bulbs they may not flower properly. Buds can fail to open if the compost is kept too dry; leaves may turn yellow if plants are grown in a draught, not enough light or low temperatures; long, limp leaves may be due to a lack of light or keeping forced bulbs in the dark for too long; deformed flowers are often the result of keeping the bulbs too warm during the forcing period; rotten flowers are due to overwatering or keeping the compost too wet; stunted growth is due to not keeping the bulbs in the dark for long enough.

Index

Acknowledgements

The majority of the photographs in this book were taken by Tim Sandall, with the assistance of David Sarton, apart from the images on pages 39 and 93, which were supplied by Jaap Westland – Huizen, Holland.

Thanks also to Coolings Nurseries for their continued cooperation and assistance with the photography in this book, including the loan of tools and much specialist equipment. Special thanks go to: Sandra Gratwick. Coolings Nurseries Ltd., Rushmore Hill, Knockholt, Kent, TN14 7NN. Tel: 00 44 1959 532269; email: coolings@coolings.co.uk; website: www.coolings.co.uk.